The Ritual Kiss
in Early Christian
Worship

by L. Edward Phillips
Union College, Barbourville, Kentucky

THE ALCUIN CLUB and the GROUP FOR RENEWAL OF WORSHIP (GROW)
The Alcuin Club, which exists to promote the study of Christian liturgy in general and of Anglican liturgy in particular, traditionally published a single volume annually for its members. This ceased in 1986 but resumed in 1992. Similarly, GROW was responsible from 1975 to 1986 for the quarterly 'Grove Liturgical Studies'. Since the beginning of 1987 the two have sponsored a Joint Editorial Board to produce 'Joint Liturgical Studies', of which the present Study is no. 36. There are lists on pages 39-40 in this Study, and further details are available from the address below. Both also produce separate publications.

THE COVER PICTURE
is a photo of the sculpture 'Das Wiedersehen' by Ernst Berlach and is taken from Albert C. Moore, *Iconography of Religions: An Introduction* (Fortress Press, 1977). It is reproduced here by permission.

First Impression December 1996
ISSN 0951-2667
ISBN 1 85174 333 2

GROVE BOOKS LIMITED
RIDLEY HALL RD   CAMBRIDGE   CB3 9HU

CONTENTS

ABBREVIATIONS

PL   *Patrologia Latina* (J. Migne)
JTS   *Journal of Theological Studies*
ANF   Ante-Nicene Fathers
ACW   *Ancient Christian Writers*

ACKNOWLEDGMENTS

I wish to thank the liturgy faculty at the University of Notre Dame, in South Bend, Indiana, especially Dr. Paul F. Bradshaw, who made many comments on an earlier version of the material contained in this book, and the late Dr. Niels Rasmussen, who introduced me to the topic of the early liturgy. I also wish to thank my wife, Sara, for her support and encouragement. And, finally, I wish to thank my students at Union College in Barbourville, Kentucky, who have listened with surprising good humour to my ruminations about kissing in the early church.

1. Socio-Cultural Background

This study investigates the developments in the use and meaning of the ritual kiss (i.e. the 'holy kiss' or 'kiss of peace') from the New Testament period through to the fifth century.

The kiss involves the senses of touch, taste, and smell, and probably has its origins in primitive human behaviour, since similar behaviours of licking, sniffing, and touching with the mouth can be found in many animal species. Examples of the kiss occur in the literature and artwork of Europe and the Middle East from very ancient times, and from then until the present, the kiss has served two related functions: communication and the delineation of social boundaries.

The kiss communicates affection or sexual desire, but it also involves the sharing or communication of breath and saliva. Modern cultures approach the exchange of bodily excretions as a potential for communicating disease. Similarly, ancient cultures conceptualized the exchange as potential for pollution of the *pneuma*. Such a fear of pollution of *pneuma* would appear to underlie Paul's concerns about sexual immorality in I Corinthians.[1] Moreover, the kiss could also function as a communication of spiritual power or other qualities contained within the *pneuma*. Thus, the kiss had a place in ancient magic[2], and examples of the kiss as a means of making or breaking enchantments can be found in the folklore of virtually every culture in the western world.

The Hellenistic Jewish romance *Joseph and Asenath* provides a rich description of this understanding of the kiss as spiritual communication. Because the kiss held the possibility of spiritual contamination, and Joseph did not allow himself to kiss Asenath before her conversion: 'And Joseph said, "It is not fitting for a man who worships God . . . to kiss a strange woman who will bless with her mouth dead and dumb idols and eat from their table bread of strangulation . . ." '[3] However, after Asenath undergoes a religious transformation through an encounter with an angel of God, Joseph can give her a kiss: 'And Joseph kissed Asenath and gave her spirit of life, and he kissed her the second time and gave her spirit of wisdom, and he kissed her the third time and gave her spirit of truth.'[4] Here, the kiss communicates spiritual qualities or powers.

In the Greco-Roman world, the *pneuma* of an individual was thought to contain the life-force or soul, and breathing in the last breath of a dying person through a kiss was thought to capture their soul.[5] This decidedly un-biblical understanding of 'soul' can be found in Jewish and Christian sources: In the *Testament of Abraham* the death angel robs Abraham of his soul through a kiss[6]; St. Ambrose gives an account of blowing into his dying brother's mouth to receive his last breath[7]; even as late as the sixth century C.E. the Council of Auxerre prohibited the kissing of the dead, considering it to be a pagan superstition.

Perhaps because of the potential for the communication of both spiritual pollution and spiritual power, the kiss was regulated in Greco-Roman cultures. According to the fifth century B.C.E. historian Herodotus, in Persia, equals in social rank kissed on the mouth,

---

[1] See Dale B. Martin, *The Corinthian Body* (New Haven, 1995) 168-174.
[2] For examples, *Greek Magical Papyrus* 1.54ff in H. D. Betz, *The Greek Magical Papyri in Translation* (Chicago, 1986) 5.
[3] *Jos. Asen.* 8.5.
[4] *Jos. Asen.* 19.11, trans., *Old Testament Pseudepigrapha* 2, ed., J. H. Charlesworth (Garden City, N.Y., 1983) 233.
[5] *Daphnis and Chloe* 1.30; *Aeneid* 6.684f.
[6] *Test. Abra.* 5.78.
[7] *De excessu fratris sui Satyr* (*PL* 16.1353).

those socially close but unequal on the cheek, and the social inferior kissed the feet of a person of higher social rank.[1] Similarly, some Roman emperors conferred the honour of kissing the emperor's face upon certain respected friends.[2] The closer persons were in social rank, respect, and friendship, the closer they were allowed to approach the mingling of *pneumata* through a kiss on the mouth.

The privacy of the family was the context within which the kiss could be shared with impunity. Greek and Roman parents kissed their children and grandchildren, and married couples kissed. The kinship kiss in the Greco-Roman world could be expanded to include a wide circle of relatives. This was significant because such kisses between related women and men did not necessarily imply incest, which was strongly prohibited.[3] In *Joseph and Asenath*, Joseph states the limits of the family kiss: 'But a man who worships God will kiss his mother and the sister (who is born) of his mother and the sister (who is born) of his clan and family and the wife who shares his bed . . .'[4] The publicly-given betrothal kiss functions in this context as a contract to establish a kinship relationship between a man and woman. But ordinarily in Greco-Roman cultures, kissing between relatives was done in private, and public displays of affection were considered improper, and perhaps illegal.[5] In Jewish society, according to Genesis Rabbah all public displays of the kiss were considered obscene except for greetings after a long absence and at partings, or in the acceptance of high office.[6]

Erotic kisses can be found in abundance in Greco-Roman literature, both heterosexual and homosexual. Yet, despite the many examples of erotic kisses, public and private sexual behaviour in the Greco-Roman world was regulated by both custom and law. Even among the more sexually liberated, the pretence of public chastity was usually maintained.[7]

---

[1] *History* I, 134.
[2] So notes the historian Arrian (1st-2nd c., C.E.), *Ammianus Marcellinus* 22.9.13, who claims that the practice was begun by Alexander, in *Alexandri Anabasis* 7.11.1.6f.
[3] Mary Pharr, 'The Kiss in Roman Law' in *The Classical Journal* 42 (1947) 393f.
[4] 8.6.
[5] Pharr (394) cites a story by Plutarch in which a senator was expelled from the senate for kissing his wife in broad daylight.
[6] *Gen. Rab.* 70.12.2. See Louise M. Epstein, *Sex Laws and Customs in Judaism* (New York, 1948) 105.
[7] As Peter Brown notes: '[T]he evidence . . . gives little support to the widespread romantic notion that the pre-Christian Roman world was a sunny "Eden of the unrepressed".' (*The Body and Society*, (New York, 1988), 21).

2. The Kiss in the New Testament

As noted above, Greek, Roman, and Jewish societies approved the kiss only in controlled circumstances, between family members or close friends, and promiscuous or public kissing even among family members was generally disapproved, if not condemned. Yet, despite these prohibitions, by the late second century C.E. the kiss clearly had an important place in the ritual life of Christians, and it was given openly in communal worship. The New Testament period is crucial for the development of this unconventional practice as Christian ritual. Unfortunately, references to kisses in the N.T. are rather few and ambiguous.

A. THE PAULINE EPISTLES

Paul uses the term *philema hagion* in the closing greetings of four of his letters: Rom. 16.16, 1 Cor. 16.20, 2 Cor. 13.12, and 1 Thess. 5.26. The phrasing of these greetings is strikingly parallel: 'Greet one another (*or* 'all the brothers', *1 Thess.*) with a holy kiss.' This phrase has been interpreted by exegetes as either: a) a liturgical rubric directing the assembly to engage in the ritual kiss; or b) a form of letter-greeting directing a customary exchange between family and close friends.

The majority of commentators assume that, as Paul's letters were read in public worship, Paul is referring to the kiss of peace such as we find in later liturgical references.[1] Among those who find a liturgical reference, J. A. T. Robinson draws attention to parallels between 1 Cor. 16.20f and liturgical material in *Didache* 10.5, even though the *Didache* contains no obvious reference to a kiss.[2] Similarly, G. J. Cuming argues for a more or less fixed sequence of 'service endings' in the letters, which concluded the 'word service' of the early church.[3] Cuming's analysis of the letters, however, requires a loose interpretation of both the order and content of the 'service endings'. Furthermore, the examples he cites for comparison are fourth century or later, and he does not demonstrate why the N.T. letters must reflect liturgical practice of the first century. One could just as well argue that the use of the epistles in worship influenced the pattern of later service endings without themselves being 'liturgical' at all.[4] Finally, Cuming does not explain the presence of other non-liturgical phrases which surround the 'service endings', such as Paul's personal handwritten addenda.

K. Thraede argues against the position that the kiss is a liturgical rite, demonstrating from a form-critical perspective that the kiss greeting is equivalent to the other friends' greetings in the letters.[5] According to Thraede, Paul surely did not expect all of the personal greetings to be read aloud wherever the letters circulated, and it is unlikely that he expected the kiss greeting to be extracted from the other greetings which surround it. Thraede proposes that the kiss was a greeting custom that later developed into a liturgical rite. Likewise, T. Mullins analyzes the form of the Greek letter greeting and suggests that the kiss in Paul's letters fits that form.[6] According to Mullins, the form for the greeting is: a. greeter (which may be implied); b. greeting verb; c. person(s) greeted; and d. elaborating phrase(s). Mullins argues that the phrase *en philemati hagio* fits into the 'elaborating phrase'

---

[1] See J. l. White, *Light from Ancient Letters* (Philadelphia, 1986) 19.

[2] 'Traces of a Liturgical Sequence in 1 Corinthians 16.20-24' in *JTS* 4 (1953) 38-41. Apart from the kiss, the parallels are notable: curse, *Maranatha*, Amen.

[3] 'Service Endings in the Epistles' in *New Testament Studies* 22 (1976) 110-113.

[4] On the problem of 'reading back' later liturgical practices into the N.T., see P. Bradshaw, *The Search for the Origins of Christian Worship* (Oxford, 1992) 35-6.

[5] K. Thraede, 'Ursprünge und Formen des "Heiligen Kusses" im frühen Christentum' in *Jahrbuch für Antike und Christentum* [1]1-12 (Münster, 1968-1969) 124-180.

[6] T. Y. Mullins, 'Greetings as a New Testament Form' in *Journal of Biblical Literature* 87 (1968) 418-426.

slot as a 'modifier'. Thus, the holy kiss 'is clearly a greeting from the writer to the third parties, with the readers of the letter as agents.'[1]

As plausible as the form-critical argument appears, it has a fatal flaw: requests for a greeting kiss are not to be found in Greek or Latin letters before the N.T.[2] Neither Thraede nor Mullins explain how a letter-writing 'convention' almost non-existent in the rest of the Greco-Roman world appears four times among the seven undisputed Pauline epistles, and once more in I Peter.

A more satisfactory solution would be to understand the *philema hagion* as a ritual which is not liturgical, *per se*, but rather as a distinctively Christian act which was shared among Christians in various times of meeting. Worship would only be one of several venues for this rite.

If Paul understood the holy kiss as a Christian ritual, it is still unclear what he meant by the term. As a phrase, *philema hagion* is quite peculiar. Why a 'holy' kiss? For Paul, the word *hagios* denotes the things that belong to God, and it often has a pneumatological aspect to it.[3] Thirteen times in the seven letters *hagia* is used with *pnuema*, the 'Holy' Spirit. The scriptures are 'holy' (Rom. 1.2), as is God's law (Rom. 7.12). Israel, as the people of God, is the 'holy' root of the tree on to which Gentile converts are grafted (Rom. 11.16). *Hagios* also describes what is acceptable before God in a cultic sense. God's temple is 'holy' (1 Cor. 3.17); the bodies of Christians are to be 'holy' sacrifices before God (Rom. 12.1); and unmarried women are urged to be *hagia kai to somati kai to pneumati* (1 Cor. 7.34). Indeed, Paul refers to Christians as *hoi hagioi*.[4] Given Paul's use of the word *hagios* elsewhere, the *philema hagion* may indicate a kiss that denotes or communicates holiness, i.e., is 'consecratory', similar to the use of the kiss in *Jos.Asen.* mentioned above.[5] The meaning of the holy kiss for Paul, therefore, is not likely to be found in his use of greetings, but in his use of consecratory language and his use of blessings, which are within his pneumatology.

Other clues indicate that the kiss has a pneumatological significance for Paul. Of the seven letters which are generally acknowledged by New Testament scholars to be authored by Paul, three do not have the kiss (Galatians, Philippians, Philemon), but they do have other parallels:

Rom. 16.16ff—Greet (*aspasasthe*) one another with a holy kiss. All the churches of Christ greet you (*aspazontai humas*). (other greeting, etc.) 16.20—The grace of the Lord Jesus Christ be with you. 16.25-27—Now to him who is able to strengthen you according to my gospel and the preaching of Jesus Christ, according to the revelation of the mystery which was kept secret for long ages . . . to the only wise God be glory for ever more through Jesus Christ. Amen.

1 Cor. 16.20-24—All the brethren greet you (*aspazontai humas*). Greet (*aspasasthe*) one another with a holy kiss. I, Paul, write this greeting with my own hand. If any one has no love for the Lord . . . Marana tha. The grace of the Lord Jesus be with you. My love be with you all in Christ Jesus. Amen.

---

[1] Mullins, 426.

[2] See F. X. J. Exler, *The Form of the Ancient Greek Letter: A Study in Greek Epistolography* (Washington, 1928). Thraede cites only one possible parallel in a letter of Cicero (*Att.* 3.16).

[3] *Theological Dictionary of the New Testament* 1,s.v. *agios*, 100-110.

[4] By which he indicates that Christians are 'pure' and therefore separate from the Gentiles (I Thess. 4.3-8). See W. Meeks, *The Moral World of the First Christians* (Philadelphia, 1986) 128f.

[5] W. Klassen suggests 'If the Christians at Philippi and elsewhere were to be greeted as "saints", the "holy kiss" is nothing more than the kiss which the saints give each other when they meet.' However, he admits he has no idea why Paul would urge this practice. See 'The Sacred Kiss in the New Testament: An Example of Social Boundary Lines' in *New Testament Studies* 39 (1993) 134.

2 Cor. 13.11—Finally, brethren, farewell. Mend your ways, heed my appeal, agree with one another, live in peace, and the God of love and peace will be with you. Greet (*aspasasthe*) one another with a holy kiss. All the saints greet you (*aspazontai humas*). The grace of the Lord Jesus Christ and the love of God and the fellowship of the Holy Spirit be with you.

Gal. 6.18—(no concluding greetings) **The grace of our Lord Jesus Christ be with your spirit, brethren** (*meta tou pneumatos humon, adelphoi*). Amen.

Phil. 4.20-23—To our God and Father be glory for ever and ever. Amen. Greet (*aspasasthe*) every saint in Christ Jesus. The brethren who are with me greet you (*aspazontai humas*). All the saints greet you (*aspazontai humas*), especially those of Caesar's household. **The grace of the Lord Jesus Christ be with your spirit** (*meta tou pneumatos humon*).

1 Thess. 5.25-28—Brethren, pray for us. Greet (*aspasasthe*) all the brethren with a holy kiss. I adjure you by the Lord that this letter be read to all the brethren. The grace of our Lord Jesus Christ be with you.

Phile. 23-25. Epaphras, my fellow prisoner in Christ Jesus, greets *you* (*aspazontai se*), and so do Mark, Aristarchus, Demas, and Luke, my fellow workers. **The grace of the Lord Jesus Christ be with your spirit** (*meta tou pneumatos humon*).

Thraede points out that the greetings in these letter closings alternate between the imperative (*aspasasthe*) and the indicative (*aspazontai*). Within this alternating pattern, he assumes that the command to greet with a holy kiss is simply another way of expressing friendly greetings and is equivalent to the command in Philippians: 'Greet (*aspasasthe*) every saint in Christ Jesus', where the kiss does not appear.[1]

However, a closer examination shows that another pattern is also present. The three letters which do not have the greeting kiss have the stereotypical blessing, 'The grace of the Lord Jesus Christ be with your spirit.' These are the only three of Paul's letters to have this blessing with this precise phrase attached. Significantly, the phrase *meta tou pneumatos humon* is found only in Christian literature; moreover, Paul, as far as there is record, is the first to use the phrase.[2] In the New Testament apart from Paul, it appears once more in 2 Timothy in the form *meta tou pneumatos sou*. The Epistle of Barnabas concludes with the phrase, but it is not used in the letters of Ignatius. The remaining occurrences of the phrase are in liturgical texts.

Paul, of course, also uses similar wording for other concluding blessings: 'The grace of our Lord Jesus Christ (etc.) be *meta humon*.' However, the blessing *meta humon* appears in all four of the letters which have the 'holy-kiss' greeting, and only there; while the blessing *meta tou pneumatos humon* appears in all three of the letters which do not have a kiss, and only there. In other words, Paul uses either a greeting kiss or a blessing *meta tou pneumatou humon* in his letters, but never both. Could it be that Paul somehow understands the holy kiss to be alternative and equivalent to the phrase 'with your spirit'?

First it must be considered whether the phrase 'with your spirit' is merely a way of saying 'with you'. Most commentators on the Pauline passages assume that the two forms have the same meaning and are interchangeable. A few scholars, however, have maintained that in virtually every instance Paul uses *pneuma* to indicate the Divine Spirit. According to this position, even when the *pneuma* has an anthropological referent, this is still to be understood as God's *pneuma* given to the believer.[3]

---

[1] Thraede, 128-9.

[2] This is confirmed by a computer search of the corpus of Greek literature in the *Thesaurus Linguae Graecae*. See also H. Ashworth, 'Et Cum Spiritu Tuo' in *The Clergy Review* 51 (1966) 122-130.

[3] See the brief review of literature in M. E. Isaacs, *The Concept of Spirit: a Study of Pneuma in Hellenistic Judaism and Its Bearing on the New Testament* (London, 1976) 70ff.

W. C. Van Unnik, in an investigation of the phrase *Dominus vobiscum*, argues that the response 'and with your spirit' is pneumatic reference.[1] He compares the *Dominus vobiscum* to blessings in the Old Testament which acknowledge God's presence with a special individual. The 'Lord' refers to the dynamic activity of God's Spirit at work in the person. For Christians, this special presence of God is not limited to a few, but rather is the gift of the Holy Spirit to the entire community. The declaration 'The Lord (is) with you' is a statement of 'fact' and refers to the manifestation of the Lord in the gift of the Spirit. The response of the congregation is the declaration that the 'Lord' (the Holy Spirit) is also with the minister, the 'spirit' being the Spirit of God which the minister has: thus, 'your Spirit' means 'the Spirit God has given you'. Referring to Paul's use of the phrase, Van Unnik comments: 'Is "with thy spirit" here the same as "with you"? . . . One may say there is identity, but not in the sense "thy spirit"="thyself", but that "you" are the Christians, i.e. men and women endowed with the Spirit'.[2] The fact that Paul is the first to use the phrase *meta tou pneuma humon*, and that he uses it in a direct blessing rather than a dialogue, supports Van Unnik's hypothesis.

What, however, could be the relationship between 'holy kiss' and 'with your spirit?' Why would Paul not use the two phrases together? There is no obvious reason for this in the epistles.[3] One possible explanation for his alternating the two phrases is that if the kiss were given along with a 'with-your-Spirit' blessing, then it would be redundant for Paul to include both in his letter-endings. In terms of their place in the letter, they would be more or less equivalent, and both phrases would indicate the practice of ritual kissing. Later, of course, the *Dominus vobiscum* and response became connected to other liturgical actions besides the kiss. Still, if the response was connected to the kiss, this would help to explain its origin in Christian practice. At any rate, the phrase appears for the first time, like the holy kiss, in the letters of Paul and by that time may already represent standard Christian usage.

The kiss, therefore, communicates more than Christian affection. Among those who have the Spirit of Christ, it would be a communication of that Spirit. Unfortunately, this evidence for a connection between the kiss and *pneuma* in Paul remains very ambiguous. The hypothesis must be examined further to see whether it fits with Paul's understanding of *pneuma*.

One striking feature of Paul's pneumatology is that he understands the Holy Spirit to be the Spirit of Christ. He indicates this in Rom. 8.9: 'But you are not in the flesh, you are in the Spirit, if in fact the Spirit of God dwells in you. Any one who does not have the Spirit of Christ does not belong to him.' This also is the meaning of 2 Cor. 3.17: 'Now the Lord is the Spirit, and where the Spirit of the Lord is, there is freedom.'[4] While is it possible for Paul to distinguish between the Spirit of Christ and the Spirit of God, for example in the Trinitarian benediction at the conclusion of 2 Corinthians, in most cases he seems to use the terms interchangeably. In this respect Paul is close to a Johannine understanding of the connection of Christ to the Spirit.[5]

---

[1] W. C. Van Unnik, 'Dominus Vobiscum' in *Sparsa Collecta*, pt. 3, *Supplements to Novum Testamentum* 31 (Leiden, 1983) 362-391.

[2] Van Unnik, 381. Note also I Cor. 14.32 where Paul states that the *pneumata* of prophets are subject to the prophets, that is, under their control. These *pneumata* are the manifestations of the divine *pneuma* which Paul discusses in I Cor. 12.4-11. Clearly, here, Paul demonstrates the close identification that he makes between the believer's *pneuma* and the divine *pneuma*.

[3] Evidence for the relationship of the phrases, however, can be found in the baptismal liturgy of *The Apostolic Tradition* where a kiss is exchanged with the *Dominus vobiscum* dialogue. See discussion below.

[4] Note a parallel in Phil. 1.19; cf. Acts 16.7.

[5] Isaacs 122.

Paul understands the Spirit to be the agent which unites the believers with God. In 1 Cor. 6.15-17 he compares union with God to sexual union with a prostitute: 'Do you not know that your bodies are members of Christ himself? Shall I then take the members of Christ and unite them with a prostitute? Never! Do you not know that he who unite himself with a prostitute is one with her in body? . . . But he who is united with the Lord becomes one spirit with him.' Paul's illustration is quite graphic: sexual intercourse with a prostitute unites the believer's body with hers. Nevertheless, the union of the believer with God is the dominant reality. This is accomplished by the Spirit which unites believers into 'one body' through baptism.[1] The ethical consequences of uniting with a prostitute is not that the believer thereby loses the Spirit, but rather that the body of Christ has been united with the prostitute, thus polluting the body of Christ.[2] Indeed, in this example, union with a prostitute is made to be analogous to union with the Lord.

Another important feature of Paul's pneumatology is his use of the relational concept of the Spirit dwelling *in* the believer: God's love has been 'poured into our hearts through the Spirit which has been given to us' (Rom. 5.5); the 'Spirit of God dwells in' the believer (Rom 8.9); the believer is the 'temple' in which God's Spirit dwells (1 Cor. 3.16).[3] In this respect Paul is again close to the Johannine notion of the Spirit[4] and quite distinct from the pneumatology of the synoptic Gospels and Acts, where the Spirit does not generally dwell within the believer,[5] but, rather, descends upon the believer. In Acts, the Holy Spirit is 'poured out' upon believers, sometimes through the laying-on-of-hands. The Pauline notion of 'indwelling' is quite different.

While Paul identifies the divine *pneuma* with the spirit of Christ, he also connects it with the *pneuma* of believers. In 1 Cor. 5.3-5 he tells the Corinthians that he is 'present *en pneuma*' though absent in body, and asks them to excommunicate an immoral church member: 'When you are assembled, and my spirit is present, with the power of our Lord Jesus, you are to deliver this man to Satan . . .'(v. 5). He also refers to the spirits of others: a virgin's *pneuma* is to be devoted to the Lord with her body (1 Cor. 7.34), and he urges the Corinthians to avoid that which contaminates the body and *pneuma* (2 Cor. 7.1). He commends them for the 'refreshing' of Titus' *pneuma* (2 Cor. 7.13). Yet, for Paul, this human *pneuma* is bound up with the divine *pneuma*, for 'we have not received the Spirit of this world, but the Spirit who is from God . . .' (1 Cor. 2.12). In 1 Cor. 15.45-49, he contrasts the creation of the first Adam *eis pseuchen zosan* (a reference to Gen. 2.7) with the last Adam *eis pneuma zoopoioun*. It is the 'Spirit' which gives life, and this is part of the new creation, not the old.

There can also be a false *pneuma*. He warns the Corinthians to avoid 'receiving a different spirit' from the one they received from him (2 Cor. 11.4). Therefore, when Paul bids the grace of the Lord Jesus Christ, *meta tou pneumatos humon*, he is not using the phrase generally, but specifically: their *pneuma* is the one they received from God through him, and not any other.

---

[1] D. Lull has raised an objection to the conventional view that the Spirit is imparted to the believer through baptism. Rather, Lull argues, the Spirit is imparted through the proclamation of the gospel, citing Gal. 3.2: 'Did you receive the Spirit by works of the law, or by hearing with faith?' Lull's view has not received wide acceptance, though it raises a valid criticism of the hypothesis that the Spirit is given by the act of baptism. Lull rightly points out that Paul nowhere explicitly states that the Spirit is given in baptism, I Cor. 12.13 notwithstanding. See *The Spirit in Galatia: Paul's Interpretation of Pneuma as Divine Power*, SBL Dissertation Series 49 (Ann Arbor, 1980) 53-59.

[2] Martin, 178.

[3] See also: Rom. 2.29; 1 Cor.; 2 Cor. 1.22; 3.3; Gal. 4.6.

[4] cf. John 3.24 and 4.13.

[5] Though note Acts 7.55 (Stephen is full of the Holy Spirit at his martyrdom) and 9.17 (Paul is filled with the Holy Spirit). However, Acts presents these as special cases.

This spirit is an indelible possession of the body of believers, but not of the individual Christian. In the passage cited above, 1 Cor. 5.3-5, Paul calls for the excommunication of an immoral man so that his *pneuma* (the portion of the *pneuma* he shares) may be saved. To be excommunicated is to be cut off from the life-giving spirit which the Christian community alone possesses. This understanding of *pneuma* also makes sense of the curious passage in 1 Cor. 7.14: 'For the unbelieving husband is consecrated (*hegiastai*) through the believing wife', and *vice versa*. Although the *pneuma* is not explicitly mentioned here, it is reasonable to assume that it is the holy *pneuma* in the believing spouse which effects the consecration of the unbeliever. Thus, the reprobate loses the *pneuma* when separated from the community, and the unbelieving spouse receives the effects of the *pneuma*, through physical association alone. Physical contact with the community is the crucial factor.[1] The unity of the Christian community is, thus, not an ethical unity, but a spiritual unity effected through the communication of *pneuma*.

For Paul, therefore, the *hagion pneuma* is the Spirit of Christ which is contained in the members of the Christian community as the body of Christ. Moreover, the *pneuma* effects a dynamic connection among believers. To share in this *pneuma* is to share in the life of Christ; to be cut off from this *pneuma* is to be condemned to destruction.

It may be suggested, therefore, that the 'holy kiss' for Paul was a ritual enactment of the sharing of the *pneuma* among believers that delineated the boundaries of the community, much in the way that the kiss could delineate family boundaries.[2] While this kiss would have been a part of the community worship of the church, it would not be limited to that context. In the letters, it would have been Paul's way of expressing his spiritual presence among the recipients of his letter, since the *pneuma* they share is the *pneuma* which he also has. This interpretation of the holy kiss would help explain how the kiss became an initiation rite in some parts of the Christian world by the second century. If the kiss is a communication of the *pneuma*, then the first kiss of the newly-initiated would understandably have taken on special significance. Moreover, this relationship of kiss and *pneuma* would greatly simplify the interpretation of Paul's notion of the 'indwelling *pneuma*'. The *pneuma* dwells within because it is communicated through the mouth of one believer to another. Finally, such an interpretation of the relationship of the *pneuma* to the believer would also make sense out of Paul's otherwise enigmatic remark in 1 Cor. 12.13: 'For by one Spirit we were all baptized into one body—Jews or Greeks, slaves or free—and all were made to drink of one Spirit.'[3] Quite simply, the *pneuma* enters the believer through the mouth.[4]

To summarize the argument: 1) Even though the term *philema hagion* is otherwise unprecedented, Paul assumes that his readers know what he means by the term and gives no indication that they would be reluctant to engage in it; 2) The use of the word *hagion* suggests a pneumatological significance; 3) a close investigation of the letter-endings indicates an apparent relationship between *the philema hagion* and *meta tou pneuma humon*,

---

[1] Martin 218f,

[2] This notion of family (brothers and sisters) is more than a mere metaphor for the early Christians. It supersedes even blood relations (Matt. 10.35). See W. Meeks, *The Moral World of the First Christians* (Philadelphia, 1986) 129.

[3] For the drinking as a metaphor for the kiss in the O.T. cf. Cant. 7.10.

[4] Bultmann points out that Paul refers to the Spirit as 'non-worldly material or as borne by such...and therefore is bound to a locality.' However, he also asserts that this 'notion of the Spirit as a material is not one that is really determinative for Paul's concept of the Spirit.' (*Theology of the New Testament*, trans. K. Grobel [New York, 1976] 333-334). The interpretation of Paul put forth above suggests, rather, that the Pauline concept of the Spirit, which Bultmann wants to interpret existentially, is quite basically a sort of 'stuff.' See Martin 277n81; A.Y. Collins, 'The Function of "Excommunication" in Paul' in *Harvard Theological Review* 73 (1980) 251-263.

suggesting that the blessing was said at the giving of the kiss; 4) an examination of uses of *pneuma* in Paul's letters further suggests that the holy kiss was a ritual communication of the divine *pneuma* dwelling within Christians. Though this last suggestion cannot be demonstrated conclusively, it does offer a comprehensive explanation of the evidence that is available. There is nothing in the letters which refutes the hypothesis, and it has the added benefit of explaining some otherwise enigmatic passages.

B. THE GOSPEL OF JOHN

As noted above, Paul's understanding of the Spirit is similar to that in the Gospel of John. Though John contains no explicit reference to a kiss, Jesus' giving of the Holy Spirit to his disciples through a breath possibly demonstrates a kiss.[1] St. Augustine suggests this image in his Sermo XLII (*De Eliszeo*): *Os enim quodam modo super os posuit, quando insufflando Spiritum dedit*. Since there are no earlier patristic references to this 'breathing' of Jesus as a type of kiss, such an interpretation could not have been a common one. Nevertheless, the story itself remains highly suggestive of a kiss; indeed, much more suggestive than typical exegetical treatments allow.

The key passage in the Greek text is verse 22: *kai touto eipon enephusesen kai legei autois: labete pneuma hagion*. The word *enephusesen* (third person, singular, aorist of *emphusao*) is difficult to translate precisely. This is the only occurrence of the word in the New Testament. W. Bauer states that with a dative object the word means 'breathe upon'. In the Septuagint, *emphusao* is the word used in Ezekiel 21.31 (quoted also in 1 Clement 39.6), clearly meaning 'breathed upon'. Consequently, John 20.22 is usually translated 'he breathed upon them'. On the other hand, with the accusative object *emphusao* may be translated 'to blow into,' as to blow into a flute. This also is the preferred translation in Genesis 2.7 (Septuagint) when, during the creation of the man, God *enephusesen eis to prosopon autou pnoen zoes*.

The Johannine passage, it must be noted, does not supply an object at all in most extant manuscripts.[2] The *autois* which is the object of *legei* appears to do double duty supplying an inferred object for *enephusesen*. The Nestle-Aland text is content to allow this ambiguity to stand as it does in the majority of the surviving manuscripts, which may imply that 'breathed upon' is the correct translation. However, there are difficulties with this assumption. Since at least the fourth century exegetes have recognized the parallel between John 20.22 and Genesis 2.7, where the verb in Greek clearly means 'breathed into'. John Chrysostom, in one sermon, actually borrows from Genesis 2.7 in his quotation of John 20.22: *Kai palin en tois Euaggeliois ho Christos proskalesamenos tous mathetas, enephusesen eis ton prosopon auton; Labete Pneuma hagion*.[3] Furthermore, both the Sahidic and Bohairic versions of John supply the prepositional phrase *ehoyn hen pey-ho*, (into their face . . .), borrowed from the Genesis passage. It is possible that a version of the Greek text of John existed which used this phrase, but that is not particularly important. What is important it that in the fourth century, John 20.22 was understood to mean 'breathed into' rather than 'breathed upon', *per se*.[4] This would lend support to the interpretation of Augustine; the giving of the Holy Spirit in John is very much like a kiss.

---

[1] So suggest N. Perella *The Kiss Sacred and Profane* (Berkeley, 1969), 18; and, S. Benko, *Pagan Rome and the Early Christians* (Bloomington, Indiana, 1986) 82.

[2] Barclay M. Newman and Eugene A. Nida, *A Translator's Handbook on the Gospel of John* (London: United Bible Societies, 1980) 615.

[3] *De jejunio* 60.722.

[4] Note F. F. Bruce translates the passage, 'breathed into...' in his commentary, *The Gospel of John* (Grand Rapids: Eerdmans Publishing Co., 1983) 391.

John 7.37-9 connects the giving of the Spirit with still another image, drinking: 'Jesus stood up and proclaimed, "If any one thirst, let him come to me and drink. He who believes in me, as the scripture has said, 'out of his heart shall flow rivers of living water'." Now this he said about the Spirit which those who believed in him were to receive; for as yet the Spirit had not been given, because Jesus was not yet glorified.' This passage anticipates the giving of the Spirit in John 20 by the exalted Jesus. R. Brown identifies this living water with wisdom typology as well as Spirit typology.[1] The Gospel of Thomas logion 108 lends confirmation to Brown's analysis: 'Jesus said, "He who will drink from my mouth will become like me. I myself shall become he, and the things that are hidden will be revealed to him".' In the Gospel of Thomas, drinking from Jesus' mouth is a symbol for receiving of gnosis, just as the living water in John refers to receiving of spirit.

Drinking the living water, thus, imparts the Spirit in a sacramental way that is at least evocative of baptism due to the water metaphor. Yet, Jesus gives the Spirit, not through drinking baptismal water (as Brown clearly sees), but through drinking in of his 'breath'. Such a sacramental interpretation of John 7.37-38 places it close to 1 Cor. 12.13, where Paul is here referring to the giving of the Spirit at baptism through the metaphor of drinking. The connection of John 7.37-38 to John 20.22 is clear: the Gospel writer himself says that Jesus is referring to the Spirit '. . . which those who believed in him were to receive' (7.39). Thus, R. Bultmann interprets John 20.22 as a transfer of spiritual power, such as we find in other ancient religions, folk tales, and magic.[2] In a more recent study, D. Parrott has suggested an even stronger reading, that in John 20.22 Christ 'breathes himself out' in the form of his 'spiritual essence'.[3] If the Holy Spirit is for John the powerful, holy breath of Jesus, then perhaps John 20.22 functions as a sort of 'institution narrative' for what Paul calls 'holy kiss'.

C. OTHER NT REFERENCES

Luke-Acts refers to kisses in several contexts. Luke 7.36-50 describes the anointing and kissing of Jesus' feet by a woman during a meal at the home of Simon the Pharisee. Here Jesus praises the woman's tender action, and chastises Simon for not offering him a kiss. G. Dix points out this passage as evidence for the kiss as a part of Jewish meal hospitality.[4] Dix's suggestion, however, is hardly tenable given the fact that none of the many other references to meals in the N.T. make any mention of a kiss, nor is there any extra-biblical evidence for a kiss in Jewish meal etiquette.

Acts 20.17-37 describes Paul's farewell address to the Ephesian elders, at the conclusion of which they prayed and 'embraced Paul and kissed him'. Again, this would have been an acceptable form of farewell bidding for very close friends or family, but it is unusual here as Luke describe the scene. Curiously, the kiss follows a prayer, which becomes an established pattern, at least in the western church, by the mid-second century. It is as least possible that Luke is describing a ritual pattern.

---

[1] R. Brown, *John 1-12*, The Anchor Bible 29 (Garden City, New York, 1966) 328.
[2] Rudolf Bultmann, *The Gospel of John*, trans. G. R. Beasley-Murray, *et al*, (Philadelphia, 1971) 692. For support, Bultmann cites G. Leeuw: 'The [ritual] kiss...was probably intended as a reciprocal transference of the breath-soul and as an exact parallel of blood brotherhood.' (*Religion in Essence and Manifestation*, Vol. 1, trans. J. E. Turner (New York, 1963) 227-8).
[3] D. M. Parrott, 'First Jesus Is Present, Then the Spirit: An Early Christian Dogma and Its Effects' in J. E. Goehing *et al*, eds., *Gospel Origins and Christian Beginnings* (Sonoma, California, 1990) 128.
[4] *The Shape of the Liturgy* 105-110. Dix wants to find the origin of the kiss of peace in Jewish meal practice.

The remaining example of a kiss in the Lukan corpus is the betrayal kiss of Judas, which Luke shares with the other synoptics. The kiss of Judas, while being an important feature of the betrayal of Jesus, is nonetheless enigmatic. As E. Schweizer asks bluntly, 'Would it not have been adequate for Judas to point his finger at Jesus?'[1] While betrayal kisses are not unknown in ancient literature, ordinarily they would be used to distract the victim or to mask evil intentions[2], but that could not be what the Gospel writers intend here, since Judas appears with a crowd of officials carrying clubs and swords. Several commentators have indicated Judas' kiss was the standard greeting between student and rabbi.[3] However, there is little evidence that first-century Judaism had such a custom, and at any rate, it does not appear to have been common.

If the kiss was communication of the Holy Spirit for some Christians, where did this practice originate? It did not originate in Jewish ritual, nor in Greco-Roman. It would seem, therefore, that the ritual kiss is distinctly Christian and arose in the original community of disciples around Jesus as a sign of their unity with him, a unity which made brothers and sisters of persons unrelated by blood.[4] This would explain the kiss of Judas— and why the early church remembered the betrayal kiss as such a heinous violation of trust, and it would explain how the kiss could later be understood as a part of initiation into the church, as was the case in some areas.

---

[1] *The Good News According to Mark*, trans. Donald H. Madvig (Richmond, Virginia, 1970) 317.
[2] For example, Joab's Kiss in 2 Sam. 20.9.
[3] D. E. Nieneham, *The Gospel of St. Mark* (Penguin Books, Ltd., Baltimore, 1963) 395; Martin Dibelius, 'Judas und der Judaskuss,' in *Botschaft und Geschichte*, Vol. 1 (Tübingen, 1953) 276.
[4] So suggests Klassen, 128f.

3. The Kiss in the Second and Third Centuries

By the second and third centuries, the evidence for the ritual kiss is more abundant and the kiss appears in a variety of contexts.

A. THE *APOSTOLIC TRADITION* OF HIPPOLYTUS

The *Apostolic Tradition* of Hippolytus (*Ap. Trad.*) dates from the early third century, which is roughly in the middle of the period to be surveyed, and exhibits the kiss in several contexts which will provide a schema with which to examine the kiss in other patristic sources.[1]

The first context in which a kiss occurs in the text is the ordination of a bishop. It comes after the ordination prayer and before the offering:

> And when he has been made bishop, all shall offer the kiss of peace, greeting him because he has been made worthy. Then the deacons will present the offering to him . . . [and here follows the opening dialogue for the anaphora].

The peace is given to the new bishop by 'all', meaning 'all the faithful'. The Latin version reads *pax*, but since the Sahidic version states more clearly, 'peace with the mouth' there is no doubt that a kiss of peace is indicated.[2]

The next kiss occurs in Ch. 18, which describes the instructional meetings for the catechumens, both women and men. The initiated members of the church also attend these daily meetings, which end with blessings and prayers. Ch. 18 specifically indicates the manner in which this diverse assembly is to pray:

> When the teacher has finished giving instruction, let the catechumens pray by themselves, separated from the faithful, and let the women, whether faithful or catechumens, stand by themselves in some place in the church when they pray. And when they have finished praying, they shall not give the Peace, for their kiss is not yet holy. But let only the faithful greet one another, men with men and women with women; but the men shall not greet the women.

The praying community is strictly segregated, catechumens from the faithful, and men from women. The arrangement is a little unclear, but it appears that *Ap. Trad.* directs the assembly to pray in four separate groups: men apart from women, and catechumens apart from the faithful. Note that the catechumens cannot give the kiss of peace because their kiss 'is not yet holy'.

The third place where the kiss occurs is in the initiation ritual in Ch. 21. Following the baptism, which has taken place in a baptistery separate from the worshipping assembly,

---

[1] The standard critical text is B. Botte, *La Tradition apostolique de saint Hippolyte, Essai de reconstitution*, Liturgiewissenschaftliche Quellen und Forschungen 39 (Aschendorffsche Verlagsbuchhandlung, Münster, 1963). The English translation is G. J. Cuming (ed.), *Hippolytus. A Text for Students*, Grove Liturgical Study 8 (Bramcote, Notts., 1976). There is no need to discuss here the problem of authorship, though this is far from settled. The widely-accepted date ca. 215 C.E. is also problematic. Several studies, including my own 'Daily Prayer in the *Apostolic Tradition* of Hippolytus' in *JTS* 40 (1989) 389-400, have argued that the document is composed from several sources, and that the received versions demonstrate layers of material later than 215 C.E. See Allen Brent, *Hippolytus and the Roman Church in the Third Century* (E. J. Brill, Leiden, 1995).

[2] Only fragments of the original Greek survive, and the text must be reconstructed from various versions, the Latin and Coptic versions being the most useful here.

the newly-baptized are brought into the meeting of the faithful for a laying-on-of-hands and final anointing by the bishop.

And the bishop shall lay his hand on them and invoke, saying: Lord God, you have made them worthy to receive remission of sins through the laver of regeneration of the holy Spirit: send upon them your grace, that they may serve you according to your will: for to you is glory, to Father and Son with the holy Spirit in the holy Church, both now and to the ages of ages. Amen.

Then, pouring the oil of thanksgiving from his hand and placing it on his head, he shall say: I anoint you with holy oil in God the Father almighty and Christ Jesus and the holy Spirit.

And having signed [Bohairic reads *sphragis*, 'sealed'] him on the forehead, he shall give him a kiss [Bohairic, *efti phi erof*, shall give a kiss to him] and say: The Lord be with you. And he who has been signed shall say: And with your spirit.

So let him do with each one. And then they shall pray together with all the people: they do not pray with the faithful until they have carried out all these things. And when they have prayed, they shall give the [kiss of] peace.

This lengthy description of initiation describes two kisses. The first kiss is given during the actual initiation by the bishop after the baptism, laying-on of hands, and final anointing. The second is the general kiss of peace which the congregation exchanges at the conclusion of prayers.

In these extracts from *Ap. Trad.*, the kiss occurs in what appear to be three distinct contexts: the ordination of the bishop, at the conclusion of prayer, and rites with the newly-baptized. The terminology for the kiss does not appear to be fixed. The Latin *pax*, clearly a translation of the Greek *eirene*, is the most common term. Sometimes 'peace' is used with 'mouth' to indicate how the kiss is to be given. However, the actual phrase 'kiss of peace' does not appear. The closest parallel is in Ch. 18 where the catechumens cannot give the 'peace', because their kiss is not yet holy. The kiss the bishop gives to the newly-baptized is called plainly 'a kiss', while the kiss that the newly-baptized share with the faithful is called 'peace with the mouth'. Given the variety of terms and contexts, it must be considered whether these kisses are related, and if so, how?

Two of the kisses come at the conclusion of prayer, although the larger context for these kisses is quite different. The new Christian shares the peace with the faithful for the first time after initiation at the conclusion of the prayer of the faithful. Ch. 18 indicates that the catechumens are not allowed to pray with the faithful until after initiation. If catechumens are not allowed to pray with the church and are dismissed just after the word-liturgy, it makes sense that they would not be present to share in the kiss. *Ap. Trad.* does not indicate whether the catechumens were *always* dismissed from the assembly before prayers, or, for that matter, whether they were ever present at a eucharistic assembly. Still, from the descriptions of the catechumenate, it is reasonable to assume that the catechumens were present for the liturgy of the word, at least during the final weeks of their preparation. In the daily catechetical instructions they are not dismissed from the assembly, but are merely required to segregate themselves from the faithful during the prayer and kiss.[1]

According to Ch. 18, the reason that the catechumens cannot share in the kiss is because their kiss is 'not yet holy'. Even within their own ranks catechumens cannot give the peace, though they are allowed to pray together. If *Ap. Trad.* establishes a pattern that prayers of the faithful are always followed by a kiss (as we shall later see is the case for Tertullian), this is not simply a custom related to prayer. Rather, it has to do with what fully-initiated Christians have that others do not, namely, a kiss which is holy.

---

[1] The catechumens are also to sit apart during the Agape meals in Ch. 27.

Ap. Trad. uses 'holy' and derived terms in a fairly consistent way. Most often the adjective is used for the Holy Spirit (nineteen times), and it also designates the holy church (seven times). *Ap. Trad.* contains other phrases which employ the word: 'holy people', 'holy things', 'holy offering', 'holy flock', etc. These phrases are found most often in the various prayer texts. Foods and oils are 'sanctified' by the prayer of the bishop, that is, made 'holy' for special purposes. Holiness indicates the presence of God, or things that have been made holy by the presence of God. For example, the breath and saliva of the Christian are holy because they contain the Holy Spirit and can be used to ward off the 'Adversary'.[1]

For *Ap. Trad.*, as for the letters of Paul, a kiss that is 'holy' would not merely indicate a kiss that is performed in a 'chaste' manner. 'Holiness' does not designate an ethical quality, but rather a 'pneumatical' quality. This is not to say that the ethical aspect of the holy kiss is absent. The 'holy' kiss is not to be shared promiscuously: men share it with men and women with women.[2] Nevertheless, the pneumatic aspect is the most obvious feature of the term in the document overall.

The first ritual kiss for every Christian is the kiss given by the bishop at baptism. The kiss comes at the very conclusion of the initiation ritual, and the bishop is to perform the same rite with each of the newly-baptized. After this kiss they pray together with the faithful for the first time, and give the peace. G. J. Cuming notes that the first kiss, *osculum*, is not the kiss of peace, *pacem*, given following the prayers.[3] Indeed, they are different, not only because of the different terms used, but also in the way the kiss is given: the bishop alone gives the *osculum* to each one of the newly-baptized, while the *pax* is shared among all the faithful. It would seem that the baptismal kiss is not merely the first time for the newly-baptized to give the *pax*. Rather, it is the kiss given by the bishop that concludes the process of initiation and is, therefore, an initiation ritual. But, in what way does the kiss initiate?

The post-baptismal rites in *Ap. Trad.* have been the subject of much controversy concerning the giving of the Holy Spirit and whether the text contains a rite of confirmation distinct from the baptism. The debate centres around the prayer which the bishop gives during the imposition of hands. There a translation of Latin version reads thus:

> Lord God, you have made them worthy to receive remission of sins through the laver of regeneration of the holy Spirit: send upon them your grace, that they may serve you according to your will; for to you is glory, to Father and Son with the holy Spirit in the holy church, both now and to the ages of ages. Amen.

However, in place of the phrase, 'of the holy Spirit', the Coptic reads 'make them worthy to be filled with your Holy Spirit'. A. Gelston has proposed a compromise solution which takes into account all the versions of the post-baptismal prayer.[4] Through a careful comparison of the versions, he argues that the original Greek text included references to the reception of the Spirit both in the water rite and in the laying-on of hands. A helpful aspect of Gelston's proposal is his recognition that there is inconsistency in the early church regarding the giving of spirit. He cites as corroborating evidence Tertullian's *De baptismo*, Ambrose's *De sacramentis*, and the *Gelasian Sacramentary*, in which the Holy Spirit seems to be connected with both the water rite and the laying-on of hands.

However, Gelston does not go far enough in his proposal. An even more careful reading of the post-baptismal prayer in the oriental versions indicates that the prayer asks that the baptizand be made worthy to fill (or be filled) with the Holy Spirit, without indicating at

---

[1] *Ap. Trad.* Chs. 42A and 42B. Note, also, Ch. 41, where signing with spittle makes one clean for prayer. However, this passage may be a later addition to *Ap. Trad.*. See Phillips, 397.

[2] It is worth noting that the command for the assembly to be segregated according to sex is made very strongly. This may indicate that this practice was not followed everywhere.

[3] Cuming, *Hippolytus*, 20.

[4] 'A Note on the Text of the Apostolic Tradition of Hippolytus' in *JTS* 39 (1988) 112-117.

what point this 'filling' is to take place. The implication is that the filling takes place in the future—the prayer merely asks for 'worthiness'. The giving of the Holy Spirit could logically come at a later point: the final anointing, the sealing of the forehead, or the kiss. Or perhaps the whole nexus of rites were, in a sense, Spirit-conferring, and the search for a precise 'rite' by which the Holy Spirit is conveyed obscures the larger picture. In the oriental versions, therefore, it appears that the kiss is part of the 'sealing' that concludes the initiation, and, along with the other rites, imparts the Holy Spirit. The importance of this is stressed in the direction that the bishop is supposed to give the concluding kiss to each neophyte separately. As noted in the previous chapter, there is a connection between the phrase 'with your Spirit' and the 'holy kiss' in the letters of Paul. In *Ap. Trad.* the connection is made more explicit: the bishop gives a kiss with the words 'The Lord be with you' and the neophyte responds, 'And with your spirit' The new Christians, thus, are spirit-filled and can offer the responsive blessing: their kiss is now 'holy'.[1]

While it would be reading too much into the text to assume that the kiss is the only rite which was connected with the giving of the Holy Spirit, it is certainly reasonable that the kiss was pneumatic for much the same reason that we see in the Pauline and Johannine evidence. For example, in Chapters 41 and 42, *Ap. Trad.* indicates that the breath of the Christian has the power to 'sanctify' the believer and to ward off the Devil. Whether or not this holy breath of the Christian is imparted by the bishop during the post-baptismal kiss is impossible to say conclusively. Nevertheless, the pneumatological connection of the kiss to holy breath/spirit indicates that the first kiss of the bishop indeed had an important place in the initiation of the new Christian into the community of the *hagioi*.

To summarize: *Ap. Trad.* displays a ritual kiss in three contexts: 1) the ordination of a bishop, 2) the conclusion of communal prayer, and 3) the concluding initiation rite. The kisses in *Ap. Trad.*, thus, would appear to be developmentally related, and display a sort of 'protocol'. The new Christians are kissed by the bishop during the initiation rites that follow the baptism. After this, they are allowed to share in the peace that concludes the prayers of the faithful. Finally, to go full circle as it were, the whole church greets the newly-ordained bishop with a kiss. In each case the actual giving of the kiss is firmly regulated as to who should kiss whom and when, and the kiss delineates those who are Christian from those who are not.

B. THE KISS AT THE CONCLUSION OF PRAYER

The Latin-African church of Tertullian connected the kiss to prayer. In his essay, *De oratione*, Tertullian has a lengthy paragraph on the *pax*:

[Ch. 18] Another custom has become prevalent. Such as are fasting withhold the kiss of peace, which is the seal of prayer, after prayer made with the brethren. But when is peace more to be concluded with brethren than when, at the time of some religious observance, our prayer ascends with more acceptability; that they may themselves participate in our observance, and thereby be mollified for transacting with their brother touching their own peace? What prayer is complete if divorced from the 'holy kiss'? Whom does peace impede when rendering service to his Lord? Whatever our prayer be, it will not be better than the observance of the precept by which we are bidden to conceal our fasts; for now, by abstinence from the kiss, we are known to be fasting. But even if there be some reason for this practice, still, lest you offend against this precept, you may perhaps defer your 'peace' at home, where it is not possible for your fast to be entirely kept secret. But wherever else you can conceal your observ-

---

[1] *Ap. Trad.* provides the earliest example of the use of the 'Lord be with you/and with your spirit' dialogue.

ance, you ought to remember the precept; thus you may satisfy the requirements of discipline abroad and of custom at home. So, too, on the day of the Pass-over, when the religious observance of a fast is general, and as it were public, we justly forego the kiss, caring nothing to conceal anything which we do in common with all.[1]

In this passage Tertullian is chastising his readers for a practice that has become common in his church: those who are fasting have been omitting the kiss after communal prayers. Tertullian warns that such a practice calls attention to the fast, which is a violation of Jesus' command to keep such special fasts privately and without display. The passage gives several clues to the practice and meaning of the kiss for Tertullian's church.

The kiss is exchanged following prayer, not only in the assembly, but even between family members at home. Tertullian allows one to omit the kiss at family prayers during a fast because it is not possible to hide a fast from one's family, but it is clear that the normal practice would be for the kiss to be shared even there. *Ap. Trad.* displays the consistent pattern of concluding communal prayer with a kiss, but it does not indicate that this practice is followed in homes, either at the Agape meal (Ch. 25f) or in the daily prayers at home (Ch. 41).[2] The practice may have been peculiar to Tertullian's church, since there is no other reference to it in the patristic literature. However, if Tertullian commands that the kiss be given in the assembly during private fasts, he clearly agrees that sharing the kiss is inappropriate during fasts. The whole church abstains from the kiss on Good Friday, because, as Tertullian says, it is not necessary to conceal a fast undertaken by the whole church. Tertullian does not indicate why the kiss is incompatible with fasting, but three possibilities come to mind. If the kiss were connected, not to prayer *per se*, but to the eucharist, then he could be referring to fasting from the eucharist on Good Friday, and at home, fasting from the reserved bread. Another possibility is that the abstention on 'Passover' may be out of consideration of the betrayal kiss of Judas. Still another reason why the kiss is incompatible with fasting would be that something is taken in through the mouth during the kiss, namely the spirit of the other Christian.

Yet, Tertullian's opinion about this is rather paradoxical, because he also indicates that fasting and other forms of self-denial have a positive effect on the value of the *pax*. In *De oratione* 18, fasting makes the prayer of the individual more acceptable to God. This is not the only place where Tertullian extols the effects of fasting. In *De baptismo* 20, persons are urged to fast, not only in preparation for baptism, but also because fasting continues to have effect following baptism. Religious disciplines of all sorts which make prayer more acceptable also make the kiss of peace more powerful. In *Ad martyres* 1.5 Tertullian describes the martyrs as special vessels of peace.

For similar reasons those who are fasting have a special responsibility to share the kiss with their fellow worshipers. Their kiss communicates a very powerful peace. This powerful peace even is passed on to others who share in the kiss, '... that they may themselves participate in our observance (the fast), and thereby be mollified (?) (*adiuuerint*) for transacting with their brother touching their own peace'.[3] Tertullian appears to be saying that in the sharing of the kiss of peace, the benefits of this fast are passed along. Moreover, the benefits can be transmitted to other persons in the assembly. Tertullian, thus, appears to have contradictory views of the kiss in relation to fasting: on the one hand, the kiss of peace is inappropriate during fasts; on the other hand, fasting makes the kiss of peace more powerful.

---

[1] Trans. *ANF.*

[2] Only at midnight is there mention of husband and wife praying together, and there is no reference to a kiss here. See *Ap. Trad.* Ch. 41.

[3] ut ipsi de nostra operatione participent, qui eam adiuuerint de sua pace fratri transigendus.

Whatever effect the kiss of peace had on those who shared it, Tertullian connects the kiss with prayer, calling it the 'seal' (*signaculum*) of prayer. The use of the word 'seal' for the kiss is intriguing. In the *Apologeticum* 21.2 circumcision in the Old Testament is the *signaculum corporis* that marked the Hebrew man. In *Ad Iudaeos* 10.1, Jesus is the 'seal' of the Old Testament prophets. The 'seal' of the cross on forehead is the sign of Christ in *Ad Marcionem* 3.22.7. More importantly, baptism is a 'seal', which in *De spectaculis* 4.1 he calls the *signaculum fidei*.

The kiss at the end of prayer may be said to have a 'sealing' significance because prayer has a pneumatological aspect: 'We are the true adorers and the true priests, who, praying in spirit, sacrifice prayer in spirit, a victim proper and acceptable to God . . .'[1] The condition for offering this 'spiritual sacrifice' is being in peace with God and fellow-Christians: 'For what sort of deed is it to approach the peace of God without peace, the remission of debts while you retain them?'[2]

How does a kiss seal the prayer? Just as baptism seals, completes faith, so the kiss of peace completes the prayer, demonstrating the united force of the prayer: 'What prayer is complete if divorced from a holy kiss?'[3] What is this uniting force? Tertullian provides a clue in *Apology* 39.1-2: 'We meet together as an assembly and congregation, that, offering up prayer to God as with united force, we may wrestle with him in our supplication. Such power God delights in.' Later in the same treatise he comments, 'They are counted and called brothers who have been led to the knowledge of God as their common Father, who have drunk in one spirit of holiness (1 Cor. 12.13) who from the same womb of a common ignorance have agonized into the same light of truth.'[4]

So firm is the connection between prayer and the kiss of peace, that Tertullian instructs Christians to pray with Christian house guests before their departure in order to share with them the peace: 'You will not dismiss a brother who has entered your home without prayer . . . how will you—according to the precept—say "peace to this house", unless you exchange mutual peace with them who are in the house?'[5] Furthermore, he well knew that this put Christians at odds with the pagan world. He comments in *Ad uxorem* on the difficulties encountered by Christian women with pagan husbands: 'Who will suffer her to creep into prison to kiss a martyr's bonds? Nay, truly to meet any one of the brethren to exchange the kiss?'[6]

To summarize, Tertullian viewed the kiss as the bond of Christian fellowship, the communication of the peace of God among those who have a common Father using the very lips which have 'drunk in one Spirit of holiness'. It is the seal which brought to completion Christian prayer made by the assembly so that their prayers may arise to God with united force.

Two other sources of this period mention the kiss at the conclusion of prayer. A few years before Tertullian, Justin Martyr, in *I Apology* 65, notes that the prayer of the faithful is concluded with the *pax* in his description of a baptismal Eucharist. A few years after Tertullian, Origen in Alexandria comments on the kiss at the conclusion of prayer in *Commentary on Romans* 10.33.

In summary, *Ap. Trad.*, Tertullian, Origen, and Justin Martyr provide unambiguous evidence that in the pre-Nicene period, the kiss was the rite by which Christians in Egypt and in the West concluded their common prayers. There is no early evidence from the eastern church.

---

[1] *De orat.* 28.
[2] *De orat.* 11.
[3] *De orat.* 18.
[4] *Ap. 39.9*
[5] *De orat.* 26.
[6] *Ad uxor.* 2.4.2-3.

C. THE KISS OF THE NEWLY-BAPTIZED

As indicated above, *Ap. Trad.* emphasized the kiss given by the bishop to each newly-baptized Christian as the last rite of the baptismal ritual. It may also be significant that the worship described by Justin Martyr refers to the kiss at the conclusion of prayers before the eucharist which followed a baptism, but not in his description of the typical Sunday service.

The evidence for a baptismal kiss in Tertullian is ambiguous. In *De baptismo* 6.1 he informs us that the Holy Spirit is not given in the water itself, but rather that the water prepares one for the Holy Spirit. *De bap.* 7.1 describes the unction which takes place immediately after coming up from the font; 8.1 describes the laying-on of hands. At this point in the ritual, the Holy Spirit is only invited upon the baptizands, but is not recognized yet as having completely filled or descended upon them. Tertullian describes the actual descent of the Spirit with reference to Christ's own baptism: the Spirit descends as a dove: *columbae figura*. Just a dove was a sign of peace in the Genesis flood story, the Holy Spirit as a dove of peace flies around the font and brings us the peace of God: *columba sancti spiritus aduolat pacem dei* (8.3).

The sequence for Tertullian would be: baptism, anointing, laying-on of hands, the descending of the dove of peace which is the Holy Spirit. Tertullian does not say that this descent of the Spirit-dove of peace is signified by a ritual kiss of peace. On the other hand, what else could he mean? Tertullian uses the word *pax* to signify the kiss of peace in *De orat.* 18. In that place and others noted above, he indicates that the peace is something shared between Christians as a special sign of the unity. In his critique of an 'heretical' group, Tertullian states that this kiss of peace is only to be shared between Christians in good standing, and that it is used as a sign of reconciliation for the lapsed. How could he refer to the *pax dei* in this context, without meaning the sign of that *pax*? It would be difficult to see how his readers would fail to make the connection.

Cyprian of Carthage plainly associates the kiss with baptism in his *Epistle* 64 written by him on behalf of the council of bishops to Fidus, a fellow bishop. The letter deals with several issues, including the giving of peace to lapsed Christians. However, the bulk of the letter deals with the practice of infant baptism. Fidus has taken the position that infants ought not to be baptized until they are eight days old, after the Jewish custom of infant circumcision. Cyprian rules against this practice, because 'the mercy and grace of God ought not to be denied to any one, even the newborn'. He uses the example of Elisha's healing of the widow's infant son to make his case.[1]

In the next section of the letter, Cyprian indicates the real reason that Fidus does not want to baptize newborn infants:

> We now turn to your claim that the foot of an infant (*vestigium infantis*) in the very first days after his birth is not clean, every one of us still recoiling in repugnance at the thought of kissing it (*exosculari*). In our view this too ought to be no reason for blocking the bestowal of heavenly grace. For it is written: To the clean all things are clean. Nor should anyone of us shudder in repugnance at that which God has deigned to make. The infant may indeed be still fresh from its birth; yet he is not such that anyone should shrink in repugnance from kissing him in the course of bestowing grace and conferring peace upon him. When we kiss an infant, piety should tell each one of us that we ought to be thinking of the very hands of God from which that infant has so freshly come; in a sense, therefore, in a human being recently formed and newly born we are kissing those hands of God when we embrace what God has made.[2]

---

[1] Epistle 64.3. Cf. 2 Kings 4.32-35. Elisha not only prostrates himself on the boy, but also breathes into him to restore life, an action similar to a kiss.

[2] Trans. G. W. Clarke, *The Letters of St. Cyprian of Carthage, ACW* 46 (Newman, New York, 1986) 111.

Fidus' objection to kissing infants is quite clear. Babies recently born are still considered unclean. Yet, Cyprian does not compromise: baptized infants are not to be denied the grace given through the kiss just because they are not appealing recipients. Rather, one should understand the newborn infant as a human being freshly made by God's own hands.

The more important feature of Cyprian's argument is his connection of the baptism to an episcopal kiss. The kiss is the sign that imparts heavenly grace and imparts peace to the newly-baptized. Just as in Tertullian's description of the kiss following prayer, Cyprian's post-baptismal kiss communicates something real. Indeed, if one were to look for a rite of imparting the Holy Spirit in Cyprian, that rite would surely include the episcopal kiss. However, is this kiss of the infant different from a kiss given to an adult convert or believer? The Latin text is ambiguous: the word 'kiss' (*exosculari*) could refer to either 'foot' (*vestigium*) or 'infant' (*infantis*). G. W. Clarke suggest the kiss was given on the foot, even though there is no other evidence apart from this letter to support such an interpretation.[1] Given the lack of supportive evidence, this position cannot be accepted. Cyprian's point in the letter is that infants need to receive the grace of God, just as adults do. It would be illogical to expect that the kiss given to an infant would be different from that given to an adult. Cyprian's reference to the feet of the infants would seem to be a euphemism for the lower body of the infant, such as we find in numerous Old Testament references.[2] Thus, the problem for Fidus is not specifically the kissing of feet, but the general uncleanness of infants, especially those newly-born.

D. THE KISS AS THE SIGN OF RECONCILIATION

The Christians who had fallen away during times of persecution were reinstated to the full communion of the church by the *pax*. This term is ambiguous, since the word alone could mean a truce, a declaration of reconciliation by the bishop, not necessarily implying a kiss. In *Ep.* 57.5, Cyprian writes on behalf of his fellow bishops to the bishop Cornelius during the Decian persecution (249-52 C.E.) stating that the peace is not to be withheld from those who are facing martyrdom, 'lest the sheep entrusted to us by the Lord be demanded back from our mouth (*ore nostro*) by which we refuse peace.' Moreover, in *Ep.* 59.13 he remarks that heretical bishops rob Christians of the true peace with 'the lie of the false peace; the salutary embrace of the mother (*salutaris sinus matris*) is shut out by the stepmother.' To receive and give *pax* was the duty of the faithful as a sign of Christian fraternity; for neophytes or the penitents it had to be conferred or renewed. For those who continued in the faith, the kiss of peace prefigured the reward of heaven in which the faithful receive and enjoy 'the embrace and kiss of the Lord (*complexum et osculum Domini*).'[3] While Cyprian nowhere states explicitly that the *pax* of reconciliation is a kiss on the mouth, the evidence strongly implies this, at least for North Africa.

E. THE ABUSE OF THE RITUAL KISS

Though the ritual kiss was the 'holy' kiss, and this meant at very least that it was chaste or undefiled, there are witnesses to the abuse of the rite. Tertullian comments on the promiscuous kissing in a certain gnostic sect, which indicates that he believed the kiss had a libertine aspect for some 'heretical' Christians.[4] There are indications that the practice of

---

[1] Clarke, 'Cyprian's Epistle 64 and the Kissing of Feet in Baptism' in *Harvard Theological Review* 66 (1973) 147-152. The closest parallels Clarke finds are in footwashing rituals.
[2] Cf. Isaiah 6.2 and Ruth 3.7.
[3] *Ep.* 6.4. See *Ep.* 37.3.
[4] *De prae. haer.* 41.3.

the ritual kiss had problematic aspects for the 'Great Church' as well. In *Ap. Trad.* Ch. 18, the strong admonition for men and women to stand apart and not to kiss those of the opposite sex most likely indicated that a more 'promiscuous' practice was the case among some Christians known to the writer. Indeed, the practice in Tertullian's church was for Christians to kiss each other as brothers and sisters, without regard for gender, and Tertullian recognized that this could lead to abuse, or to the appearance of abuse.[1]

The first writer to address an actual abuse of the kiss in the worshipping assembly is Athenagoras:

> We think it is of great importance that those, whom we think of as brother and sister or family, ought to maintain their bodies undefiled and uncorrupted. For again the word says to us, 'If anyone kiss a second time (*tis dia touto ek deuterou kataphilaesae*) because it brings pleasure . . .' Therefore, the kiss, or rather the salutation, should be given with the greatest care, since, if there be mixed with it the least defilement of thought, it excludes us from eternal life.[2]

Athenagoras appears to be quoting some other source, though he does not say what that source is. His point is that the kiss shared between Christians ought to be a kiss between siblings rather than between lovers. If Christian 'brothers and sisters' kiss each other a second time, the kiss has become a vehicle for physical enjoyment. When the holy kiss becomes an erotic kiss, it is dangerous, and can even exclude the Christian from the reward of eternal life. Similarly, Clement of Alexandria gives warning about the abuse of the ritual kiss:

> . . . [Love] is not proved by a kiss, but by kindly feelings. But, there are those that do nothing but make the churches resound[79] with a kiss, not having love itself within. For this very thing, the shameless use of a kiss, which ought to be mystic, occasions foul suspicions and evil reports. The apostle called the kiss holy. When the kingdom is worthily tested, we dispense the affection of the soul by a chaste and closed mouth, by which chiefly gentle manners are expressed. But, there is another, unholy kiss, full of poison, counterfeiting sanctity. Do you know that spiders, merely by touching the mouth, afflict men with pain? And often kisses inject the poison of licentiousness. It is then very manifest to us, that a kiss is not love.[4]

Clement is concerned that the kiss be kept holy in practice. The kiss is not a sign of agape unless chaste love is exemplified among those of the assembly. The kiss itself is not love and can be dangerous if not kept chaste. Similarly, Tertullian refers to the practice among Christian women of kissing the chains of the confessors in prison as an embarrassing problem[5], and Cyprian indicates that some of the confessors had, in fact, engaged in sexual intercourse with women while still in prison.[6] Charges of libertinism against Christians are as old as the New Testament itself.[7] In the second and third centuries, 'orthodox' Christians charged various gnostic Christian sects with sexual immorality, and pagans lodged such complaints against Christians of all varieties. Whether or not there was some factual basis for this in actual Christian practice is a much-debated question. Clement himself indicates that the Carpocratian gnostics practiced sexual libertinism.[8] Therefore, it is significant that in the *Paedagogus*, Clement indicates there was reason for evil reports in the practice of his own community. In response to this abuse, Clement sets firm limits on

---

[1] *Ap.* 39.
[2] *Sup. chris.* 32.3, trans. *ANF*.
[3] *katapsupheo.* The word means to make an inarticulate sound, perhaps a loud smacking noise.
[4] *Paed.* 3.12, trans., *ANF*.
[5] *Ad usor.* 2.4.5.
[6] *Ep.* 13.5; *Ep.* 14.3.
[7] S. Benko, *Pagan Rome and the Early Christians* (Bloomington, 1986) 54-78.
[8] *Stromata* 3.2.11.

the practice of the kiss: it is to be performed with a 'chaste, closed mouth'. Every effort should be made to ensure that the ritual kiss was not confused with an erotic kiss.

F. THE SECOND AND THIRD CENTURIES: CONCLUSION

In the second and third centuries, the kiss appears at the conclusion of prayers (in the worshipping assembly and in more informal settings), in the baptismal ritual, and in rituals of reconciliation. What seems to be lacking is any definite evidence connecting the kiss of peace to the eucharist, since the kiss was performed as the conclusion of the prayers of the faithful, rather than as a preparation for the Eucharist itself.

We have argued that the kiss was understood as a rite which actually communicated the Spirit. Even the kiss at the conclusion of prayers was not merely a sign of fellowship, but of spiritual unity among the faithful who continue to share the Holy Spirit with each other. It would seem, therefore, that despite the many contexts in which it occurred, there was only one type of ritual kiss for the early church, and that was the holy kiss which united them in the one Holy Spirit of Christ.

4. The Kiss in the Fourth and Fifth Centuries

In the fourth century and later, the kiss maintains some remnants of its connection to communal prayer and initiation, but it also becomes attached to the eucharist, either as a preparation for the eucharistic prayer or as a preparation for communion.

A. THE KISS IN EUCHARISTIC LITURGIES

By the fourth century, when evidence for the eastern liturgies appears, the kiss is found at various places in the pre-anaphoral rites. R. Taft has proposed that the variations developed because the transfer of gifts and the *lavabo* originally occurred during the exchange of the *pax*. As the transfer and the *lavabo* become formalized, the *pax* is placed at a convenient place 'before or after the *pax*, which seemed more convenient'.[1] The kiss became detached from its original place at the conclusion of the intercessory prayer in several Eastern liturgies, and became a preparation for the eucharist, as a demonstration of Matt. 5.23.[2]

In the *Apostolic Constitutions*, on the other hand, the kiss is still connected to the intercession. In the description of the eucharist in *Ap.Const.* II 57.14-21 the kiss comes after the first of two intercessory prayers, and takes place during the transfer of gifts.[3] Likewise, in *Ap.Const.* VIII 11.5-9 the kiss follows the prayer of the faithful, and comes before the *lavabo* and the transfer.

The kiss is explicitly mentioned after the prayer of the faithful before the eucharist; however, the liturgy in *Ap.Const.* VIII actually contains four distinct sets of intercessions: a) the prayer of the faithful before the offertory; b) the intercessions at the end of the eucharistic prayer; c) the litany after the eucharistic prayer; and, d) the intercessions of the prayer after communion. In a) and c) the prayer is in litany form and is led by the deacon, while in b) and d) the prayer is given by the bishop on behalf of the congregation. In all four sets, prayers are offered for the clergy, for public leaders, for the congregation, for the weather, for the harvest, and for catechumens. It is notable that the intercessions which conclude the eucharistic prayer are followed immediately by an exchange, 'The peace of God be with you all/And with your spirit', which is the same exchange we find at the kiss of peace which concludes the bishop's collect after the prayer of the faithful. *Ap.Const.* VIII indicates that the peace exchange begins the diaconal litany after the eucharistic prayer, rather than concluding the eucharistic prayer. Nevertheless, this *pax vobiscum* dialogue is possibly the remnant of a kiss which concluded the intercessions. Perhaps this 'peace' exchange accompanied these intercessions into the eucharistic prayer, but without the kiss, when intercessions were introduced there in the fourth century or earlier.

While the kiss of peace came before the eucharistic prayer in the East, in Rome and in North Africa it came after the eucharistic prayer. This is a distinguishing mark of these rites at least from the early fifth century, though, as noted above, in the second- and third-century western sources, the kiss came before the eucharistic prayer at the conclusion of the prayer of the faithful. Two questions arise: a) Why did this shift in the location of the kiss of peace occur? and, b) how early did this shift take place?

In North Africa, at least from the time of Augustine, the kiss was tied to the Lord's Prayer as an enactment of the petition to 'forgive us our debts as we forgive our debtors.'

---

[1] R. Taft, *The Great Entrance*, Orientalia Christiana Analecta 200 (Rome, 1978) 50.

[2] Cyril of Jerusalem (*Mys.Cat.* 5.3), Theodore of Mopsuestia (*Bap. Hom.* 4.40), and John Chrysostom (*Ad Dem.* 1.3) all cite this text.

[3] E. Bishop, 'Liturgical comments and Memoranda' in *JTS* 14 (1913) 50ff., notes that such an arrangement is not unusual in eastern liturgies.

In Sermo 227, Augustine gives an outline of the liturgy, and states that the kiss of peace follows the Lord's Prayer, which follows the Sacrifice:

. . . when the Sacrifice is finished, we say the Lord's Prayer (*dicimus orationem dominicam*) which you have received and recited. After this, the 'Peace be with you' is said, and the Christians embrace one another with the holy kiss (*post ipsam dicitur Pax vobiscum, et osculantur se christiani in osculo sancto*). This is a sign of peace; as the lips indicate, let peace be made in your conscience . . .[1]

After this, Augustine goes on to speak about the reception of communion. Although it cannot be ascertained how early the Lord's Prayer was placed at the conclusion of the eucharistic prayer, it is possible that the kiss was moved along with the Lord's Prayer to this location in the rite.[2] However, this need not be the case. The Lord's Prayer could have been placed at the end of the eucharistic prayer before the kiss was placed there, with Augustine merely making the connection clearer. Or, the kiss could have already been at the conclusion of the eucharistic prayer after the intercessions (a possibility suggested by *Apostolic Constitutions* VIII), and the Lord's Prayer inserted later.

Regardless of how the liturgy may have developed in North Africa, the earliest evidence of a post-anaphoral position for the kiss in the Roman liturgy comes from the letter, c. 415, of Innocent I to Decentius, bishop of Gubbio, an Italian town just to the north of Rome:

You say that certain people hold that the *pax* should be given to the people, or that the priests should give each other the *pax*, before the Mysteries are consecrated: whereas, of course, the *pax* ought to be given after the completing all those 'secret' things I may not disclose, by which it may be manifest that the congregation assents to all that is done in consecrating the Mysteries, and all that is done in the churches, and, when all is finished, they can illustrate this by the closing seal of the *pax*.[3]

It seems that Decentius knew of the ancient practice of offering the kiss of peace before the anaphora. Innocent instructs Decentius to follow the present Roman pattern, which uses the *pax* as a 'concluding seal' (*signaculum*) of the eucharistic prayer. As Dix points out, Innocent is not trying to make Decentius refrain from introducing an innovation; rather, he is attempting to induce Decentius to conform to more recently-established Roman practice.[4] While Innocent does not seem to be making an innovation himself, it is impossible to discern just how long this had been the Roman pattern. It certainly cannot be the case that Rome followed the pattern of North Africa, which linked the pax to the Lord's Prayer, since the Roman liturgy did not have the Lord's Prayer after the consecration until the time of Gregory the Great.[5]

Innocent construes the kiss as the 'seal' of the eucharistic prayer which precedes it, much as Tertullian had called the kiss the 'seal of prayer' more generally, in *De orat.* 18.

---

[1] Trans. *Fathers of the Church* 38, 197-198
[2] As suggested by Dix, *Shape*, 109.
[3] Trans., G. Ellard, 'How Fifth-Century Rome Administered Sacraments' in *Theological Studies* 9 (1948) 6. The critical edition is R. Cabié, *La lettre du pape Innocent Ier a Décentius de Gubbio* (Louvain, 1973).
[4] Dix, *Shape*, 108.
[5] In a letter to John, the Bishop of Syracuse, Gregory indicates that he is not copying Byzantine practice in putting the Lord's Prayer at the conclusion of the canon. Gregory states that the Byzantines recite the prayer aloud in the congregation, while he directs that the prayer should be recited by the priest alone.

However, Innocent's letter gives us another clue to placement of the kiss in his directions about the reading of the names in the canon:

But about reciting the names before the priest recites the [peace or prayer, *pacem or precem*], as well as before he in prayer commends to God the oblations of those whose names are to be recited: your own discretion will see how foolish it is, when you have not yet commended his oblation to God, that you should first insinuate his name to God, even though nothing be unknown to him. Therefore, the oblations are to be first commended to God, and then the names of those whose oblations they are, are to be recited. The names are thus to be recited within the sacred Canon and not among the other preparatory matter, by which we pave the way for the coming Mysteries [or, by which we pave the way by the Mysteries for the prayers to come].

The first line of this paragraph presents an important textual problem. Four different early manuscripts, three which are of the eighth century (the earliest extant copies), have the word *pacem* rather than *precem* in the first sentence. One eighth-century manuscript contains the word *pacis*. According to the critical edition, only one of the eighth-century sources has the word *precem*. R. Cabié chooses the reading *precem* because he thinks it makes more sense: the 'prayer' would be the eucharistic prayer, and Innocent is directing Decentius to read the diptychs during the canon.[1] However, Cabié's suggestion is not convincing. It would seem that it is fairly easy by scribal error to get from *pacem* to *precem*, but not from *precem* to *pacis*; therefore, *pacem* should be the preferred reading. Such a reading would connect the intercessory prayer or naming of the names with the kiss, which is, of course, the early pattern in the West. Innocent is not denying the connection between the intercessions and the *pax*; rather, he is more or less indicating that if you move one, then you move the other.

This analysis suggests that the motivation for the relocation of the *pax* is the connection of the kiss to the reading of names and other intercessory prayers which were placed within the Roman canon by the time of Innocent I. The kiss was the 'seal' of the eucharistic prayer for Innocent, just as it was the 'seal' of prayer for Tertullian, because the intercessions were, by Innocent's time, part of the eucharistic prayer.

While Innocent clearly connects the kiss to the eucharistic prayer, by the end of the fourth century another interpretation of the kiss was already making its way into the Roman understanding: the kiss of peace is connected to the reception of communion. Jerome, for example, indicates that there is no communion without the peace, though it is not absolutely clear that he means by this the kiss of peace, or some more general notion of harmony in the community.[2] Ambrose also seems to connect the kiss to the eucharist in *De sacramentis* V.5-7 when describes the Christian's approach to the altar and reception of communion employing imagery from the Song of Songs. Whatever may have been the case for Jerome and Ambrose, by the time of Gregory the Great, the kiss is no longer connected to the eucharistic prayer, but to the reception of communion. In *Dialogue* III.36, Gregory gives an account of monks on a ship who give each other the kiss of peace before they receive the consecrated host. Furthermore, the sixth-century *Rule of Benedict* stipulates that monks give each other the kiss of peace before they receive communion from the pre-consecrated bread.[3] In the West, therefore, a pattern develops that is very similar to that in the East, and as the connection between intercessory prayer and the kiss is forgotten, the kiss becomes connected to the reception of the eucharist.

---

[1] Cabié, 41f.
[2] *Ep.* 82.
[3] Benedict, *Rule*, 63.4.

B. THE KISS IN INITIATION RITES

The evidence for Roman baptismal practice in the late fourth century comes not from Rome, but from Ambrose of Milan. Ambrose was quite attracted to Roman liturgical usage, and in his catechetical sermons he often comments that the rites of Milan are similar to those of Rome, or makes apology for deviations from Roman practice. Yet Ambrose is sometimes unclear about the performance of the rites he describes, and this is often less than clear about the rites he describes, as in his description of the post-baptismal 'seal.' In *De sacramentis* Ambrose makes reference to a *spiritale signaculum* following baptism:

> The spiritual sealing follows. You have heard about this in the reading today. For after the ceremonies of the font, it still remains to bring the whole to perfect fulfillment. This happens when the Holy Spirit is infused (*infunditur*) at the priest's invocation; 'the Spirit of Wisdom and understanding, the Spirit of counsel and strength, the Spirit of knowledge and piety, the Spirit of holy fear . . .'[1]

Ambrose indicates that the 'spiritual seal' is given by the *sacerdos* (surely the bishop) to the newly-baptized. This seal comes after the post-baptismal anointing and foot washing, and it imparts the Holy Spirit.[2] The importance of the spiritual seal for Ambrose is indisputable, though he does not give us any concrete description of what sort of rite the spiritual seal entails.[3] Nevertheless, this absence of description has not stopped scholars from trying to reconstruct the ceremony. Most concur that the spiritual seal involved a sign of the cross on the forehead of the newly-baptized and perhaps an anointing.

In *De sac.* 6.6-7, which comes near the end of the lecture, after the description of the eucharist, Ambrose makes another reference to the *signaculum*:

> God anointed you, the Lord put his sign on you and placed the Holy Spirit in your heart. So you received the Holy Spirit in your heart. But there is another point: just as the Holy Spirit is in your heart, so too Christ is in your heart. How can this be? You have it in the Song of Songs, where Christ says to the church: 'Set me as a seal upon your heart, as a seal upon your arm'. God anointed you, then, Christ put his sign on you. In what sense? You were given a sign in the form of his cross and of his passion. You received the seal in his likeness to enable you to rise again in his form and live after the model of the one who was crucified to sin and lives to God.[4]

Although Ambrose does not call this seal the *signaculum spiritale*, this does seem to be the seal that he is describing, since it is the seal of the 'Holy Spirit in your heart'.

Ambrose says that God anoints and Christ (or the Lord) seals. Does this mean that the anointing is connected to the seal? The later baptismal rite of Milan does indeed have an anointing with chrism at the making of the sign of the cross after baptism, as does the Roman Rite. Yet Ambrose seems to distinguish anointing from the sealing: God anoints; Christ seals. He makes this distinction twice in the same passage. Accordingly, L. Mitchell suggests that the seal is the sign of the cross.[5]

Yet, the sign of the cross is not the only possible parallel. As suggested above, *Ap.Trad.* 21 connects the seal with a post-baptismal kiss. While Ambrose makes no explicit mention of a post-baptismal kiss, in his *Ep.* 41, he makes a reference to the kiss that is relevant for his baptismal liturgy. He is commenting on Luke 7.36-50, the story of Simon the Pharisee

---

[1] *De sac.* 3.8. Trans. E. Yarnold, *The Awe-Inspiring Rites of Initiation: Baptismal Homilies of the Fourth Century* (Slough, England, 1971). Ambrose makes a similar reference in *De mys.* 7.43.

[2] See H. Riley, *Christian Initiation*, Studies in Christian Antiquity 17 (Washington, D.C., 1974) 357.

[3] P. Jackson, 'The Meaning of *Spiritale Signaculum* in the Mystagogy of Ambrose of Milan' in *Ecclesia Orans* 7 (1990) 81. See also Riley, 353.

[4] Trans. Yarnold, 151.

[5] L. Mitchell, *Baptismal Anointing*, Alcuin Club Collections 48 (London, 1966) 88f; see also Riley, 353f.

and the woman who kisses Jesus' feet. Ambrose states that Simon could not have given a kiss since he had not received the peace from Christ. He goes on to say that the one who praises Christ gives him a kiss, as does the one who reads the Gospel, or the one who receives the *osculum communionis*, the kiss of communion. It is unclear whether this a reference to communion or to the kiss given before communion. But, Ambrose specifically refers to the reception of the Spirit as giving a kiss to Christ:

> De specialis quoque gratiae infusione eadem te Scriptura docet, quod osculetur Christum, qui accipit Spiritum, dicente propheta sancto: Os meum aperui, et attraxi Spiritum (Ps. 118.131).[1]

Ambrose states that the kiss infuses grace, and that one 'kisses Christ in receiving the Spirit'. In *De sac.* 3.8 Ambrose says that at the invocation of the bishop, the Holy Spirit is 'infused' (*spiritus sanctus infunditur*) in the newly-baptized. The use of the word *infundo* in both of these passages suggests that the seal in his baptismal liturgy involves a ritual kiss: the kiss infuses the Holy Spirit, as in *Ap. Trad.* 21.[2]

There is further evidence for a post-baptismal kiss in later Roman or western rites, though from Rome itself there are very few early sources of information after *Ap.Trad.* The Letter of John the Deacon to Senarius, a Roman nobleman, which dates from around 500 C.E., gives the next fairly detailed presentation of the baptismal ritual.[3] John mentions several post-baptismal rites: vesting in a white garment, anointing of the head with chrism, and the placing of a white cloth on the head of the neophyte. He does not mention either the second anointing or a kiss or any sort of sealing by the bishop. Still, it would be rash to conclude from this passage that John did not know of these other rites. The letter to Senarius does not purport to be a complete account of initiation. Moreover, at a later passage in the letter, John indicates that other rites were part of the ceremony, particularly the rites which are reserved for the bishop.

The next relevant evidence comes from the *Gelasian Sacramentary*, which dates from the late seventh century. A. Chavasse, in his analysis of the sacramentary, is quite willing to allow that some of the material is very ancient, and that the baptismal material is among the oldest.[4]

The *Gelasianum* also conforms to the outline of Roman baptism which is found in *Ordo romanus*, ca 650.[5]

A comparison of the four witnesses to Roman baptism indicates a remarkable consistency in post-baptismal rites from the third to the seventh century as shown in the chart on the facing page.

---

[1] *Ep.* 41.15.

[2] It is not necessary to assume that Ambrose thought that the Holy Spirit was only communicated by a kiss. P. Jackson has convincingly argued that in Ambrose's mystagogy the Spirit is imparted in the whole series of rites from the water bath to the conclusion of the ritual. The conclusion of the ritual is called the *spiritale signaculum* merely because it is the conclusion of the pneumatic sequence (the 'final seal'), not because it is the precise point at which the Spirit is given. Jackson leaves open the question of whether there was a discrete rite which accompanied the *spiritale signaculum* and functioned as a communication of the Spirit. See Jackson, 89-94.

[3] Text in A. Wilmart, *Analecta Reginensia*, Studi e Testi 59 (1933) 170-179.

[4] A. Chavasse, *Le sacramentaire gélasien* (Paris, 1958) 168.

[5] M. Andrieu, *Les ordines romani du haut moyen âge* 2, (Louvain, 1948) 417-447.

Ap. Trad.	John the Deacon	Gelasianum	Ordo XI
	1. vesting in white		
1. anointing/ oil of thanks-giving.	2. anointing of head with chrism	1. sealing on forehead with chrism/prayer.	1. sign of cross on head with chrism by presbyter.
2. putting on clothes/enter church	3. dressing of head in white linen		2. receiving of infant in towel. giving of stole, chasuble, chrismal cloth, ten coins, and robing of infant.
3. Bp. lays on hands/prayer		2. laying on of hands, with prayer for seven-fold spirit.	4. confirming with prayer for grace of seven-fold spirit.
4. anointing on head/oil of thanksgiving/ seal on forehead	4. anointing with chrism by bishop	3. Seal on forehead with chrism	5. sign of cross on forehead with chrism, in name of Trinity.
5. kiss with *Dominus tecum/et cum spiritu tuo*	5. blessing of bishop	4. *Pax tecum/et cum spiritu tuo.*	6. *Pax tecum /Amen.*

As this chart indicates, the pattern from *Ap. Trad.* to *Ordo XI* remains virtually the same. Of particular interest is the *Pax tecum* and response in the *Gelasian* rite and *Ordo XI*. The *pax tecum* is obviously parallel to the *Dominus tecum* in *Apostolic Tradition*, though there is no rubrical indication of the exchange of a kiss, as is in *Ap. Trad.* Yet, neither the *Gelasianum* or *Ordo* XI indicate that the kiss of peace is to be exchanged with the *pax* before communion. This is not an indication that the kiss was not given, but only that the *pax* dialogue was the obvious and sufficient cue for the rite.[1]

It would seem that the *pax tecum* is a remnant of the blessing which *Ap. Trad.* has at the post-baptismal kiss. This blessing is a feature of a particularly Roman type of post-baptismal rites; it is not found in eastern initiation rites, nor is it found in any of the later Gallican sources. Perhaps the disappearance of the post-baptismal kiss in the Roman rite was a gradual accommodation to the practice of the rest of the church. Nevertheless, that the kiss was once a part of the Roman initiation rite can hardly be disputed, and it is likely it was practised at least as late as the sixth century.

Eastern rites also describe a kiss following baptismal rites. The question arises whether this kiss was distinctly connected to baptism or merely the expected kiss which was given at the eucharist.

In the second baptismal instruction from the Stavronikita Series, John Chrysostom gives a description of the welcoming of the newly-baptized by the church community immediately following the water rite:

[1] J. Jungmann, *Mass of the Roman Rite*, vol. II (Trans., New York, 1955) 321.

What follows suffices to show us from what those who have been judged worthy of this mystic rite have been set free, and what they have gained. As soon as they come forth from the sacred waters, all who are present embrace, greet (*aspazontai*), kiss (*kataphilousi*), rejoice with, and congratulate [them], because those who were heretofore slaves and captives have suddenly become free men and sons and have been invited to the royal table. For straightway (*eutheos*) after they come up from the waters, they are led to the awesome table heavy laden with countless favours, where they taste of the Master's body and blood, and become a dwelling place for the Holy Spirit.[1]

As Chrysostom describes it, the reception into the church is a joyous celebration which contains, among other features, a direction for the community to kiss the newly-baptized. In the third catechetical lecture from the Papadopoulos-Kerameus Series, Chrysostom instructs the neophytes in the meaning of the kiss before the eucharist:

(32) When we are about to participate in the sacred Table, we are also instructed to offer a holy greeting. Why? Since we have been divorced from our bodies, we should join with one another on that occasion by means of the kiss, so that our gathering becomes like the gathering of the apostles when, because all believed, there was one heart and one soul.

(33) Bound together in this fashion, we ought to approach the sacred mysteries. Hear what Christ says: 'If you are offering your gift at the altar, and there remember that your brother has anything against you, go first to be reconciled to your brother and then offer your gift'. He did not say: 'First offer'; He said: 'First be reconciled and then offer.' When the gift is set before us, let us, therefore, first become reconciled with one another and then proceed to the sacrifice.

(34) But there can be another mystical meaning of the kiss. The Holy Spirit has made us temples of Christ. Therefore, when we kiss (*philountes*) each other's mouths, we are kissing (*kataphiloumen*) the entrance of the temple. Let no one, therefore, do this with a wicked conscience, with a mind that festers beneath the surface. For the kiss is a holy thing. St. Paul says: 'Greet one another with a holy kiss.'[2]

In this sermon, the kiss is connected with the eucharistic service; Chrysostom gives a common eastern interpretation of the kiss with reference to Matt. 5.23-4: the kiss is a sign of reconciliation before the offering of the Eucharist. In *Stav.* 2.27, on the other hand, the kiss can be characterized not as reconciliation, but, as a kiss of welcome and congratulation.[3]

Chrysostom, therefore, would seem to describe the post-baptismal kiss in very different terms from the kiss before the eucharist. Given the presence of two kisses in *Ap. Trad.* 21, several scholars have taken the position that Chrysostom is also referring to two distinct ritual kisses in his catechetical lectures: one a post-baptismal kiss, and the other the kiss of peace before the eucharist. J. Quasten cites the *Acta sancti Mar Abdu'l Masich* as evidence that the Syrian tradition knew a separate post-baptismal kiss. The *Acta* describes a baptism of a shepherd boy by his Christian comrades, after which they all give him a kiss. Of course, there is no eucharist, because the shepherds do not have a priest at their disposal. Yet, according to Quasten, the shepherds copy what they have seen in church, and that includes a post-baptismal kiss. Likewise, suggests Quasten, this is what Chrysostom

---

[1] *Stav.* 2.27. Critical ed., A. Wenger, *Huit catéchèses baptismales*, Sources chrétiennes 50 (Paris, 1957); trans., P. W. Harkins, *St. John Chrysostom: Baptismal Instructions*, ACW 32 (London, 1963) 53.

[2] Papadopoulos-Kerameus 3.32-34; trans., Harkins, 171-2.

[3] So it is designated by Yarnold, 34.

describes in his post-baptismal congratulatory kiss.[1] T. Finn, in his investigation of the baptismal rites of Chrysostom, agrees that Chrysostom describes a post-baptismal kiss.[2] However, Finn's study of Chrysostom's baptismal liturgy indicates a problem with this position. Immediately after his discussion of the kiss, Finn begins his discussion of the baptismal eucharist, but he does not comment on the kiss of peace which Chrysostom clearly notes is the prelude to the celebration of the eucharist. What has happened to the pre-eucharistic kiss in Finn's outline of Chrysostom's rite?

Finn has assumed a parallel between Chrysostom and the ritual kisses in *Ap. Trad.* 21: Stav. 2.27 is the post-baptismal kiss; P.K. 3.32ff is the pre-eucharistic kiss of peace. Yet, in each sermon Chrysostom mentions only one kiss. Moreover, in Stav. 2.27 Chrysostom states that immediately after the baptism, the neophytes are led to the table for the eucharist: '... straightway after coming up from the waters they are led away to the awesome table.' Despite the fact that the kisses are described in very different terms, is it really the case that the kiss in Stav. 2.27 is a distinct post-baptismal kiss?

Evidence from other Syrian baptismal suggest it is not. Cyril of Jerusalem and Theodore of Mopsuestia do not refer a post-baptismal kiss, though both of them mention the kiss of peace before the Eucharist. Neither does Pseudo-Dionysius mention any post-baptismal kiss, though he describes several other ritual kisses.[3]

The Syriac Acts of John the Son of Zebedee includes a kiss of peace in one of its accounts of baptism:

And when he had come up out of the water, then he clothed him in white garments, and gave to him the kiss of peace, and said to him: 'Peace be unto you, you new bride-groom, who had grown old and effete in sin, and lo, today are become a youth, and your name has been written in heaven.'[4]

The Syriac Acts of John is a mid-to-late fourth century work, and, thus, roughly contemporaneous with Chrysostom. This account in Acts of John is very similar to the fifth-century description by Narsai of the kiss following baptism:

As a babe from the midst of the womb he looks forth from the water; and instead of garments the priest receives and embraces him. He resembles a babe when he is lifted up from the midst of the water; and as a babe every one embraces and kisses him. Instead of swaddling-clothes they cast garments upon his limbs, and adorn him as a bridegroom on the day of the marriage-supper.[5]

New garments and bridal imagery are common to these accounts. Possibly, also, the theme of new birth in Narsai is parallel to the theme of restored youth in Acts of John. In Narsai, the bishop embraces the neophyte, while the congregation gives a kiss. In Acts of John, John gives a kiss to the neophyte. Unfortunately, one cannot tell whether other Christians would also have given a kiss, since none are present. Despite the differences, it does appear that both of these accounts connect the kiss to baptism, as does Chrysostom. However, it is also the case that neither Acts of John nor Narsai mention another kiss

---

[1] J. Quasten, 'Der Kuss der Neugetauften in altchristlicher Taufliturgie' in ed. Walter Dürig, *Liturgie: Gestalt und Vollzug* (Munich, 1963) 269-270.

[2] *The Liturgy of Baptism in the Baptismal Instructions of St. John Chrysostom*, Studies in Christian Antiquity 15 (Washington, D. C, 1967) 197-199.

[3] Thomas L. Campbell, *Dionysius the Pseudo-Areopagite: The Ecclesiastical Hierarchy* (Washington, D. C..1981). See 2.2.4 for an example of the priest kissing the altar during the baptismal rite. See 3.2 and 3.3.8 for the kiss of peace before the eucharist. For other ritual kisses see 5.3.6 (ordination); 6.3 and 6.3.4 (monastic consecration); 7.2; 7.3.4; 7.3.8 (funerals).

[4] Trans. W. Wright, *Apocryphal Acts of the Apostles*, excerpted in E. C. Whitaker, *Documents of the Baptismal Liturgy* 2nd ed. (SPCK, London, 1970), 19-20.

[5] *Hom.* 221, trans., R. H. Connolly, *The Liturgical Homilies of Narsai* (Cambridge, 1909) 52.

before the eucharist which follows. Narsai, as noted above, immediately follows the baptism with the eucharist, beginning with the *Sursum corda*.

Therefore, all three of these accounts of post-baptismal rites mention only one kiss, rather than two as in *Ap. Trad.* 21. While it would appear that there is a special baptismal interpretation of the first kiss given to the neophyte, this kiss is nothing other than the kiss which ordinarily precedes the eucharist. The fact that the kiss receives a different interpretation at baptism is not unusual, since even the first eucharist has a special significance for the newly-baptized. Note, for example, the marriage-supper theme in Chrysostom, which also applies to the kiss in both Acts of John and Narsai.

The theme of congratulations at the post-baptismal kiss which we find in Chrysostom is not unique either. It occurs in the *Canons of Hippolytus* 19:

> Next he signs their forehead with the oil of anointing and gives them the kiss saying 'The Lord be with you.'
> And those who have been baptized also say, 'And with your spirit.' He does this to each of the baptized.
> After that they pray with all the people of the faithful and they give them the kiss and rejoice with them with cries of gladness.
> Then the deacon begins the liturgy . . .[1]

The baptismal rite in *Can. Hipp.* follows *Ap. Trad.* 21 very closely, and it also has a post-baptismal kiss separate from the kiss of peace which follows the prayers of the faithful and precedes the eucharist. In Canons of Hippolytus, however, the theme of congratulations is not associated with the bishop's post-baptismal kiss, but with the kiss that the congregation gives to the newly-baptized following prayer, which is the regular kiss of peace.

Similarly, the theme of congratulations is found in Pseudo-Dionysius' account of the kiss given to those who make monastic professions:

> If, even now, the priest and all the holy men present give the kiss of peace to the one consecrated, see here the holy society of godlike men, who lovingly congratulate one another with a divine joy. At the end of all, the priest invites the consecrated person to the supremely divine Communion . . .[116]

The parallels to the baptismal rite in Pseudo-Dionysius' rite of monastic consecration are obvious. It is notable, moreover, that the kiss of congratulations given by the monks is the only kiss which is mentioned before the eucharist. This is the same pre-eucharistic kiss of peace which is described in *Ecc. Hier.* 3.2 and 3.3.8., different only in that it occurs in the specific context of the monastic consecration.

One final bit of evidence is provided in the baptismal rite in the *Testamentum Domini*, a late fourth or early fifth-century church order of Syrian origin possibly originating from Asia Minor:

> And when he seals him on the forehead, let him give him the Peace and say, the Lord God of the humble be with you. And let him who has been sealed reply: and with your spirit. And thus for each one separately.
> From that time let them pray together with all the people.
> Let the offering be received from the deacon, and let the shepherd give thanks . . .[3]

---

[1] *Can. Hipp.* 19; trans. C. Bebawi, in P. Bradshaw, *Canons of Hippolytus*, Alcuin/GROW Joint Liturgical Study 2 (Bramcote, Notts., 1987) 24.

[2] *Ecc. Hier.* 6.3.4-5.

[3] *Test. Dom.* 11.9-10; trans. G. Sperry-White, *The Testamentum Domini: A Text for Students*, Alcuin/GROW Joint Liturgical Study, 19 (Bramcote, Notts., 1991) 29.

Like *Can. Hipp.*, *Test. Dom.* is based to a large degree on *Ap. Trad.*; thus it refers to a post-baptismal kiss which the bishop gives to the neophytes. It is very curious that *Test. Dom.* does not have a separate kiss after the prayer of the faithful, as does *Ap. Trad.* Rather, *Test. Dom.* appears to be conforming to contemporary Syrian practice. For example, the prayers of the faithful are not made at this place in the Syrian baptismal rite. Though *Test. Dom.* refers to the prayers, a careful reading indicates that the prayers are not offered, but only that *from this time forth* the neophytes are allowed to pray together with the faithful. By the fifth century, it was certainly the case that the kiss of peace was no longer strongly attached to the end of the prayers of the faithful, as it is in *Ap.Trad.*, but rather to the eucharist which followed. Therefore, *Test.Dom.* gives only one kiss, because only one kiss was given in the Syrian rite, namely the kiss before the eucharist.

In summary, the evidence indicates that the Syrian baptismal rite did not have a separate post-baptismal kiss. On the contrary, the evidence indicates overwhelmingly that the Syrian church knew only one kiss, and that was the kiss that preceded the eucharist.

C. THE KISS AND ORDINATION RITES

The ordination rite in *Ap. Trad.* 4 describes the kiss given by the congregation to the newly-ordained bishop.[1] All the church orders based on *Ap. Trad.* include this congregational kiss. By the late fourth century the ordination kiss begins to develop its own distinct use. *Ap.Const.* VIII.4.10 indicates a separate kiss of the newly-ordained bishop by the attending bishops in addition to the congregation kiss.

By the fifth century there is evidence that the distinct ordination kiss was part of all ordination rites in the East. Pseudo-Dionysius' *Ecclesiastical Hierarchy* indicates that all those who receive ordination to 'any sacerdotal order,' specifically, bishop, presbyter, and deacon, are to be greeted with a kiss. The kiss concludes the ordination ceremony, and follows the sign of the cross on the forehead and the 'sacred calling of the name'.[2] This kiss, however, is given only by the other members of the clergy and the bishop, rather than by the entire assembly. Moreover, the interpretation of the kiss in *Ecclesiastical Hierarchy* is particularly linked to the clergy and is a sign of 'equals' within the ranks. Pseudo-Dionysius has a stratified vision of the assembly: the clergy are equal to the clergy and the laity to the laity. Therefore, the kiss for Pseudo-Dionysius is not a representation of Christian equality, but rather of the clerical hierarchy: it distinguishes as well as unites.[3]

---

[1] It is not clear whether this is a distinct 'ordination' kiss or a 'special' of the kiss shared by the faithful following prayer. See P. Bradshaw, *Ordination Rites of the Ancient Churches of East and West* (New York, 1990) 35. See also K. Richter, 'Zum Ritus der Bischofsordination in der "Apostolischen †berlieferung" Hippolytus von Rom und davon abhängigen Schriften' in *Archiv für Liturgiewissenschaft* 17 (1975) 32.

[2] *Eccl. hier.* 5.2.

[3] The disintegration of the kiss as a sign of equality can already be seen in *Ap.Trad.* 18 with the separation of women and men.

5. Conclusion

It is outside the scope of this study to chart the waning of the kiss of peace in Christian worship, though the kiss as a congregational act had largely disappeared by the end of the medieval period. The recent liturgical revisions in Roman Catholic and Protestant churches have advocated a return to the use of a sign of peace in worship. The contemporary practice amounts to a reclaiming of what is assumed to be early Christian practice, but with notable differences. Modern liturgical revision has substituted a 'sign of peace' for the 'kiss of peace'. Yet, is it really equivalent to substitute another 'sign' of peace for a 'kiss'? We may wonder whether a handshake or even an embrace could function in the same way. While it is highly unlikely that an actual kiss on the mouth, as attested in many patristic sources, could ever be re-introduced into modern practice, it is a mistake to assume that this was an easy matter for the early church. Christians were defying cultural norms when they kissed each other within their communities, and this provided the basis for scandal.

This study has argued that the kiss originally functioned as a means of communicating the Holy Spirit, rather than 'love' or 'peace' *per se*. Even when the pneumatological function was forgotten, the kiss served as a radical enactment of Christian unity in a way that a handshake never could: close family members shared a kiss; friends used less intimate forms of greeting. This would appear to be true in most western cultures today. Strangers may shake hands on greeting; the kiss, particularly the kiss on the mouth, is reserved for more intimate relationships. Yet, it is precisely this sort of counter-cultural family bond which the early Christians enacted in the kiss. The present practice of giving a sign of peace 'according to local custom'[1] would seem to be asking for cultural accommodation, rather than radical community.

Finally, however, we may wonder whether it is really desirable or even possible for the current practice of the sign of peace to find its rationale in the ritual kiss of the early church. The church, for instance, did not retain the pneumatological interpretation of the kiss for long. Would this not indicate that the ritual kiss simply became incompatible with the doctrine of the Holy Spirit, and, likewise, with a more developed ecclesiology?

Liturgists writing in the pastoral vein have noted problems which the sign of peace has created.[2] Some parishioners object to the sign of peace because it seems artificial to place an act of fellowship, such as a handshake, in the midst of the liturgy, especially since many people already give spontaneous handshakes before and after the service. On one level, this indicates a general misunderstanding of how ritual functions. Still, on another level, it may be that the ritual does not make sense as it is practised. Without its pneumatological meaning or its meaning as a counter-cultural demonstration of family bonds, the sign of peace may not have sufficient purpose. Perhaps it is best not to base the contemporary practice of the 'sign of peace' on the 'kiss of peace' of the early church, but to acknowledge that what we have done is to introduce a ritual into contemporary Christian practice that has very little in common with the early Christian practice of the kiss.

While it is unthinkable that the pneumatological meaning of the rite could be reclaimed (even if this were desirable) the counter-cultural notion of family could possibly be reclaimed in some congregations. The *pax* should at least retain some notion of unity and equality. Whatever sign is performed should be done consistently among worshipers without regard for kinship or friendship. In this at least something of the radical meaning of the kiss could be regained: in Christ, all Christians are sisters and brothers under the parenthood of the God whom Jesus called 'Abba'.

---

[1] *General Instruction on the Roman Missal* 112.

[2] See, for example, C. Buchanan, *The Kiss of Peace*, Grove Worship Series 80 (Grove Books, Bramcote, 1982).

THE GROUP FOR RENEWAL OF WORSHIP (GROW)

This group, originally founded in 1961, has for well over twenty years taken responsibility for the Grove Books publications on liturgy and worship. Its membership and broad aims reflect a highly reforming, pastoral and missionary interest in worship. Beginning with a youthful evangelical Anglican membership in the early 1970s, the Group has not only probed adventurously into the future of Anglican worship, but has also with growing sureness of touch taken its place in promoting weighty scholarship. Thus the list of 'Grove Liturgical Studies' shows how, over a twelve-year period, the quarterly Studies added steadily to the material available to students of patristic, reformation and modern scholarly issues in liturgy. In 1986 the Group was approached by the Alcuin Club Committee with a view to publishing the new series of Joint Liturgical Studies, and this series is, at the time of writing, in its tenth year of publication, sustaining the programme with three Studies each year.

Between the old Grove Liturgical Studies and the new Joint Liturgical Studies there is a large provision of both English language texts and other theological works on the patristic era. A detailed consolidated list is available from the publishers.

Since the early 1970s the Group has had Colin Buchanan as chairman and Trevor Lloyd as vice-chairman.

THE ALCUIN CLUB

The Alcuin Club exists to promote the study of Christian liturgy in general, and in particular the liturgies of the Anglican Communion. Since its foundation in 1897 it has published over 130 books and pamphlets. Members of the Club receive some publications of the current year free and others at a reduced rate.

Information concerning the annual subscription, applications for membership and lists of publications is obtainable from the Treasurer, The Revd. T. R. Barker, 11 Abbey Street, Chester CH1 2JF. (Tel. 01244 347811, Fax. 01244 347823).

The Alcuin Club has a three-year arrangement with the Liturgical Press, Collegeville, whereby the old tradition of an annual Alcuin Club major scholarly study has been restored. The first title under this arrangement was published in early 1993: Alastair McGregor, *Fire and Light: The Symbolism of Fire and Light in the Holy Week Services.* The second was Martin Dudley, *The Collect in Anglican Liturgy;* the third is Gordon Jeanes, *The Day has Come! Easter and Baptism in Zeno of Verona.*

The Joint Liturgical Studies have been reduced to three per annum from 1992, and the Alcuin Club subscription now includes the annual publication (as above) and the three Joint Liturgical Studies (with an extra in 1994). The full list of Joint Liturgical Studies is printed overleaf. All titles but no. 4 are in print.

Alcuin/GROW Joint Liturgical Studies

All cost £3.95 (US $8) in 1997

1987 TITLES
1. **(LS 49) Daily and Weekly Worship—from Jewish to Christian**
   by Roger Beckwith, Warden of Latimer House, Oxford
2. **(LS 50) The Canons of Hippolytus**
   edited by Paul Bradshaw, Professor of Liturgics, University of Notre Dame.
3. **(LS 51) Modern Anglican Ordination Rites** edited by Colin Buchanan, then Bishop of Aston
4. **(LS 52) Models of Liturgical Theology** by James Empereur, of the Jesuit School of Theology, Berkeley

1988 TITLES
5. **(LS 53) A Kingdom of Priests: Liturgical Formation of the Laity: The Brixen Essays**
   edited by Thomas Talley, Professor of Liturgics, General Theological Seminary, New York
6. **(LS 54) The Bishop in Liturgy: an Anglican Study** edited by Colin Buchanan, then Bishop of Aston
7. **(LS 55) Inculturation: the Eucharist in Africa**
   by Phillip Tovey, then research student, previously tutor in liturgy in Uganda
8. **(LS 56) Essays in Early Eastern Initiation**
   edited by Paul Bradshaw, Professor of Liturgics, University of Notre Dame

1989 TITLES
9. **(LS 57) The Liturgy of the Church in Jerusalem** by John Baldovin
10. **(LS 58) Adult Initiation** edited by Donald Withey
11. **(LS 59) 'The Missing Oblation': The Contents of the earlyAntiochene Anaphota** by John Fenwick
12. **(LS 60) Calvin and Bullinger on the Lord's Supper** by Paul Rorem

1990 TITLES
13-14 **(LS 61) The Liturgical Portions of the Apostolic Constitutions: A Text for Students**
   edited by W. Jardine Grisbrooke (This double-size volume costs double price (i.e. £7.90 in 1997))
15 **(LS 62) Liturgical Inculturation in the Anglican Communion**
   edited by David Holeton, Professor of Liturgics, Trinity College, Toronto
16. **(LS 63) Cremation Today and Tomorrow** by Douglas Davies, University of Nottingham

1991 TITLES
17. **(LS 64) The Preaching Service—The Glory of the Methodists**
   by Adrian Burdon, Methodist Minister in Rochdale
18. **(LS 65) Irenacus of Lyon on Baptism and Eucharist**
   edited with Introduction, Translation and Commentary by David Power, Washington D.C.
19. **(LS 66) Testamentum Domini** edited by Grant Sperry-White, Department of Theology, Notre Dame
20. **(LS 67) The Origins of the Roman Rite** Edited by Gordon Jeanes, then Lecturer in Liturgy, University of Durham

1992 TITLES
21. **The Anglican Eucharist in New Zealand 1814-1989** by Bosco Peters, Christchurch, New Zealand
22-23 **Foundations of Christian Music: The Music of Pre-Constantinian Christianity**
   by Edward Foley, Capuchin Franciscan, Chicago (second double-sized volume at £7.90 in 1997)

1993 TITLES
24. **Liturgical Presidency** by Paul James
25. **The Sacramentary of Sarapion of Thmuis: A Text for Students**
   edited by Ric Lennard-Barrett, West Australia
26. **Communion Outside the Eucharist** by Phillip Tovey, Banbury, Oxon

1994 TITLES
27. **Revising the Eucharist: Groundwork for the Anglican Communion**
   edited by David Holeton, Dean of Trinity College, Toronto
28. **Anglican Liturgical Inculturation in Africa** edited by David Gitan, Bishop of Klrinyaga, Kenya
29-30. **On Baptismal Fonts: Ancient and Modern**
   by Anita Stauffer, Lutheran World Federation, Geneva (Double-sized volume at £7.90)

1995 TITLES
31. **The Comparative Liturgy of Anton Baumstark** by Fritz West
32. **Worship and Evangelism in Pre-Christendom** by Alan Kreider
33. **Liturgy in Early Christian Egypt** by Maxwell E. Johnson

1996 TITLES
34. **Welcoming the Baptized** by Timothy Turner
35. **Daily Prayer in the Reformed Tradition: An Initial Survey** by Diane Karay Tripp
36. **The Ritual Kiss in Early Christian Worship** by Edward Phillips